Wooden Nickels

The Inside Looking Out

Terry McKoy

WOODEN NICKELS, The Inside Looking Out

Copyright ©2024 by Terry McKoy
All rights reserved.
No part of this publication may be reproduced, distributed, or transmitted in any form or by any means, including photocopying, recording, or other electronic or mechanical methods, without the prior written permission of the publisher, except as permitted by U. S. copyright law. For permission requests, contact Terry Mckoy at bearthmarkpublishingllc@gmail.com
For privacy reasons, some names, locations, and dates, may have been changed.
First Edition 2024
ISBN: 979-8-218-37066-4
United States Copyright Office ID: 1-66T3TDU

This testimony is dedicated to my mother, my three children, and my seven grandchildren.
~I love my family.

Table of Contents

Book 1		Egg & Larva	8
1	In the Beginning		9
2	Miss Cellaneous		17
3	This is Us		21
4	Sound Foundation		29
5	Best Man for the Job!		34
6	What Just Happened?		38
7	Forbidden Places		42
8	Think Differently		46
9	Wildflower		50
10	I know that was God		56
11	My Daddy, My Hero		61
12	Divine Intervention		66
Book 2		Pupa & Chrysalis	7
13	Middle School		72
14	Blip, Blip, Blip		80
15	Shhh...		84
16	The Truth Can't Lie		92
17	High School		96
18	It Keeps Happening		101
19	Firm Faith		107

20	When God Shows Up	113
21	One Prayer	121
22	For Much is Required	128
23	He'll Make it Alright	134

Book 3	Butterfly & flying	146
24	Problem	147
25	Know	154
26	Just Peachy	160
27	Ladybug	167
28	The Message	170
29	Broken Record	181
30	Exhibit A	186
31	I need you God	192
32	Do Not Assume	200
33	Who said What	206
34	Exhibit B	211
35	I Asked God	218
36	What a Friend	223
37	Imagine Me	231

Introduction

I used to assume that the ask, "Forgive them father, for they know not what they do", referred to children. I realize now that it applies to anyone who lacks enough courage required to be a representation of what God intended. They know not what they do.

"Who is God to you?"

That was the first question Pastor asked as the choir closed out the start of service. Music still played softly.

"I know who he is...I refuse to keep it to myself."

"The bible says, these... hold their peace, rocks will cry out."

Music fading...

"When we think about who God is and what God does, we want to let the world know, I know who God is." He continued, "Your story is a great part of God's story... Your story is what makes you strong.... Your story is what makes you so determined... Your story Is what makes God so great... Your story is what makes God so powerful! Your story makes you eligible to be used!"

"Note to self, if it had not been for the Lord on my side, Where...?"

"You must be the one who testifies to the world that having God changes your life."

"When these chosen strangers met God, they were searching for life, looking for hope, and looking for answers."

"They were praying for direction, and when they heard the gospel preached, they found their hope, they received their answers, and God gave them answers, and God gave them direction and so now, a few ticks off the clock later, they can testify that God changed their lives."

"There was a night and day difference."
~Pastor

When I listened to the entire sermon for the first time a few years earlier, I wasn't prepared to tell my story because I didn't know it.

That was then, and now is now.

Book 1
Egg & Larva

Chapter 1 In the Beginning

I still recall details of my earliest memory. I must have been no more than three years old; I woke up from a bad dream to a dim unfamiliar living room. I heard loud grinding motor sounds coming in through the window. I was lying on a couch that was covered in plastic and the only thing that separated me was a thin bed sheet that hung loosely just across the middle seat cushion and expanded up the back of the tall chair. I guess it was supposed to make the plastic bearable. I was hot and sticky. I looked around the whole room. I was alone. I saw a bright yellow shiny spot from the edge of the couch peeking out from beneath the thin bed sheet. The ends of the chair's arm where wooden and shaped in the form of a balled-up fist. There was matching loveseat, and single chair placed in the corner, next to the couch, both covered in fully exposed plastic. Small throw pillows were neatly placed on all the chairs. Plants were everywhere. One was so long, that it stretched along the entire perimeter of that room. The small fragile glass table showcased a small potted plant and a few magazines, while the matching end tables held small twin lamps. There was a big brown cardboard box with toys in it placed on the end table next to me. The long curtains waved wildly as the big box fan blew hot air in from outside. The curtains didn't match anything. I peeled my damp skin away from the plastic spot where the thin bed sheet escaped, sat straight up, and began to scream out loud, crying as loud as I could for Mommy.

Suddenly, she appeared. Rushing in from the other room, dressed in a thin house coat that buttoned up the front, and a huge Afro she had long fingernails that were sharp, shiny rings on two of her fingers, a golden tooth on

the right side of the gap between her front top teeth, and fuzzy slippers on her feet. She was tiny, soft spoken, and polite. She was extremely nervous approaching me, I was hysterical after all.
She tried her best to calm me down, she sat beside me, and she says "shh" ... repeatedly.
 "I'm here, I'm here, Mommy's here now."
I continued to scream. Terrified and confused, I was finally silenced with a sweet treat to eat and a drink. I was satisfied with something to eat and then I watched TV for a while. Mommy continued with her chores and attended to me accordingly. After a while, some more kids showed up. They must have been in school during my nap. They were all very excited to play with me. Mommy told me they were my sisters and brothers. I was the baby of the family.
My name is Charity Eliza Heal or 'Cherry' for short. I was a tiny thing. Very skinny legs, big bright brown eyes, very tamed cold black hair. I have very distinctive birthmarks on, of all places God could choose...my face. It's light spots and I always wondered why marks had to be on my face. I also have a few beauty moles on my face: one on the corner of my lip, and the other near my ear. I have a star in my eye too, it's a little small lump in the corner. I must have been born with bags under my eyes. They were there for as long as I could remember.

    Risha and I were not only close in age, but we were also very close in size. We started out just about the same height and then slowly I outgrew her by about an inch overtime.

    Risha had a much darker complexion than me and she had a patch on one eye when we were small because it was lazy and went its own way. When we were young, she had a surgery to correct it. She wore eyeglasses very early and she had very short coarse hair. She was also super thin like me, but we were very different in personality. Risha was quiet, and she struggled academically in school. I on the other hand, loved school, and academics was not a challenge for me. Risha repeated a few grades when we were attending elementary school, so we completed elementary school at the same time.

China was the oldest girl, the beauty queen of the three. She was oldest and she was privileged. She had different struggles all through school. For starters, there were some incorrect information on her school forms and every year her school enrollment process was delayed. In Daddy's spot, the name was someone other than Daddy. Mommy said it was an error made by the hospital people and it wasn't a big deal. Mommy had to verify her information each year until they finally got it corrected right before she went off to middle school. China would get so frustrated every school year because teachers would use the other man's last name as China's last name on the school records, and everyone knows we were the Heals. Mommy would always say, "don't worry about it, these things happen, it will all straighten out when you get married." So, we didn't.

China kept her room squeaky clean; we couldn't even sit down on her bed. When we were allowed into her bedroom, we had to sit crisscross applesauce along the wall on the floor. We didn't care, she had the best toys and the neatest bedroom decor. It was an honor to be allowed in because she had the best record player and all the latest records. China was dark complexed as well. She had a very athletic build and sort of tall for her age, I guess. Since she was older, she was involved in different things like dance class and friends at school, so she didn't spend a lot of time with Risha and me. She was regarded as mean to those who didn't know her.

Roy was the oldest of all of us and the only boy. He looked exactly like daddy, but with a rounder face shape which I learned later when I got to see daddy. He was tall and very dark. Had a big round face and a big round head, with big bright eyes like mines. He had Mommy's gap between his two front teeth. He was the pride and joy boy. Spoiled rotten and could do no wrong.

Roy was very serious about his grades when he was in school, and he enjoyed sports also. He had a lot of friends that he played with outside. They would always do cool stuff like build go karts, skateboards, or a pigeon coop. Normal boy stuff, like building a tree house, or just fixing on a bike, was my source of entertainment. Roy tried to shoo me away all the time, but I enjoyed their activities much better than what my sisters where doing. Which was nothing. He was playing basketball and baseball and football he was washing cars doing all the fun stuff. Roy had a lot of responsibilities in the house. He had to empty the trash, take care of our dog Toby, and make sure the car stayed washed. Roy was everybody's favorite because he was so much like Daddy. I guess he was just fun to watch.

My brother Roy short for Royban was the first born, China and Risha were next. We're all two years apart in age, but sometimes depending on our birthdays, Risha and I would have a slightly closer age gap.

We had a dog named Toby she was my best friend. Toby was a mostly white large mixed breed with three large gray spots on her coat. She had a small gray spot on her face right near her nose. Her eyes where big and brown and she had huge floppy ears. Toby was so smart. Toby slept in my room most nights. The cat Tracy slept in a makeshift cat bed that was formerly a baby's bathtub, could have been mines, but I'm not sure. I didn't like Tracy very much, something about her eyes really creeped me out. My sister China loved Tracy. Tracy was her best friend. I was loud and playful unlike my siblings in that way, I was different. A lot of times the joke was on me. It was normal because I was the baby, so of course I'm the "but" of the jokes.

    The house was small, with just two rooms on the first floor. It had exits in both of those rooms, so if you came in from the front of the house, you'd see the walk-in pantry known as Roy's room where we also kept a deep freezer, the washing machine, bikes, gas powered lawn mower, and the kitchen trash can. Also, the clothes drying lines for when there was inclement weather on laundry days. The threshold was draped with a floral curtain that extended from the ceiling to the floor. Right outside from that pantry, was the kitchen. Featuring a huge shallow/deep double-sided sink made of concrete, garnished with Tracy's bed nestled below it. The sink had a curtain along it as well and it matched the pantry and the window too. There was the small gas-powered stove in the corner with a handy tin can of bacon grease readily available for use at any time. The refrigerator was positioned next to the stove by a small shelf that housed silverware and coffee mugs.

    There where countless nights of defrosting the refrigerator when the ice built up so much that the food couldn't fit properly. The next room was the living room it was a big square room with that big plant that wrapped around the whole perimeter of the room, growing out of a big yellow Tupperware bowl. Mommy sold Tupperware, Sarah Coventry, vacuums, perfume, Avon, soda, frozen cups, custom designs, and salvaged goods to make ends meet. The room had one huge window. The door had jousters that could open for ventilation and a mail slot that would allow the mailman to drop the mail onto the living room floor. In the middle of the two rooms there were a set of stairs that were concrete as well. Up those steps to your left there's one adult bedroom and to the right there was the girl's bedroom, somewhere in between there's a linen closet in the bathroom. The bathroom didn't have a shower, just the bathtub, toilet, and sink. The hallway, there was a linen closet had shelves packed with towels and random sheets and curtains. I was small enough to climb on those shelves when we played hide and seek in the house. The floors were painted Gray throughout the entire house.

  Luckily, we were moving into a new house that had an extra bedroom which meant Roy wouldn't have to sleep in the pantry anymore. It was a few doors away from our current house, so on moving day we just packed everything up and walked a few doors down. The new house had three bedrooms and it was in the middle of the row, same row, same set up. In that house the girls all still shared a room. Our bedroom had a set of bunk beds finally and one full size bed for China. We had one long dresser with six large drawers arranged in three rows of two drawers and three smaller drawers across the top. It had a large, squared mirror attached to the back, making it all one piece. We all had two drawers a piece and one mini drawer for underwear. There was a window on one side of the room and right below it was the radiator. The radiator doubled as a clothes dryer in the winter months. That's where China's bed was. The bunk beds were on the opposite side of the room near the entrance. Risha had the bottom bunk because she was a heavy sleeper.

WOODEN NICKELS, The Inside Looking Out

At the foot of China bed was the closet door. We had a tiny closet with a double tiered hat rack on the top that I couldn't reach. We had matching bedspreads on all our beds that Mommy made from old clothes patched together. She attached border with little bright red cotton bells around the outside for added appeal and stuffed the inside with scraps of fabrics for fullness. They were adorable and sort after. Mommy was taking orders and making them throughout the neighborhood. We had matching curtains to top it off and accented the whole thing with a braided multicolored throw rug between our beds on the floor. China and Risha would cover their beds with stuffed animals and dolls when we weren't sleeping. I kept mines clear and free for writing tablets and cassette tapes. I had posters on the wall of poems and paintings. China had a few posters of her favorite music groups at the time. Risha just struggled to keep her bed made. I helped Risha a lot because she was quiet and shy, so she didn't ask for help, you had to pay attention. Daddy told me that.

Roy had his own room all to himself. Afterall, he was the oldest kid, and he was the only boy. We stayed in that house for few years and then we move one more time in that decade, and you've guessed it, same row same setup. This time, the houses had been through an upgrade and showers were installed in all the houses for free. Everybody also got smoke detectors and fancy radiators to replace the old metal ones with the chipped paint that made loud noises when the water inside heated up as it moved through the pipes.

We moved to the corner house this time with another extra bedroom, so now we have 4. One bedroom was on the first floor and that was our parents' room. We adjusted along the way as we got older. But growing up Risha and myself shared a room, we split the bunk beds into single size beds and mines replaced China's. Window seat for me. China had her own room, and Roy had his room to himself. We were able to paint the walls with different colors, and Mommy glued mirror tiles around the Livingroom. We were even able to put carpet on the floors. By that time, we had a little small yard and mommy planted fresh greens tomatoes and cucumbers. There was a Peach tree in the yard that grew real Peaches. You could find those trees in a few of the neighbors' yards too. We weren't allowed to play in other people's yards, we had to stay away from the fruit even if it fell on the ground. I grew up on that row of houses. Things changed a lot when we moved to that house.

Chapter 2 Miss Cellaneous

From the inside looking out, I was groomed to learn things the hard way. I mean we all played and got along well but I took risks early. I needed information but, I was treated like an invisible ghost. Instead of telling me that fire burns, they would go on and let me touch it. I felt that I had to advocate for myself since I was three. Like the time when my siblings and I were all sitting around the kitchen table, and I wanted to play Wonder Woman. I decided to prove to Roy and China that I could fly, because they couldn't make me believe that I couldn't. So, I tied a towel around my neck and let it hang down my back as my cape. I pulled the kitchen chair out from the table, planning to land square on it. They all quietly watched.
Roy snickered and shook his head as I took a head start, backed all the way up to Tracy's bed/the kitchen sink, with about 4 feet distance from my mark.

I took off with short a running start. I really ran top speed and right before I got to the chair. I jumped and I stretched my hands out in front of me, and I stretched my feet out behind me, and when I was completely stretched out, I yelled, "Wonder Womaaaan!", and I completely cleared the chair.

I crashed right into the wall headfirst! I saw a light flash. I hit my head so hard I could taste the pain. I knocked my tooth loose and I had a busted lip. All my siblings burst out laughing they thought it was the funniest thing ever. I screamed and cried I thought I wasn't going to all the way make it.

A scream from mommy echoed, as she came running downstairs yelling, "What happened!? What happened!?"

They were all laughing and yelling over top one another, "She was being silly trying to fly and supposed to been landing on a chair and missed it."
They continued falling over laughing trying to explain what happened to the baby. Mom checked me out and gave me a cookie and a cup of orange juice to ease the pain.

As Mommy cleaned me up, she said, "See, you're going to be a problem."

Food became my comfort. I mean that in a way of if I ate food, it made me feel better very early. Once my snacks kicked in, I was bragging about how I proved to them that I could fly. I ain't never say like a bird!

After dinner one typical evening, we were sitting in the living room all the siblings with Mommy, and we were looking through some shoe boxes of family pictures and picture books. We were pulling out all kinds of artifacts about everyone. You know Roy, where he was a baby. Cute pictures of China when she was a baby. Risha even had one with her footprints on it. Everybody's birth certificates and little baby pictures were nicely kept, so as we looked through all the photos one by one and it felt like there were hundreds of them, I started to notice something strange. I searched and searched and searched we all searched and searched and searched all finished searching all the photos and all the artifacts and all the albums and oddly enough we didn't find one picture of me. Not one.

I asked, "Where's my baby pictures and where's my birth certificate?"

Everybody laughed and said things like, "Oh baby girl by the time you came along we weren't even doing pictures anymore."

"Yeah, Cherry you were found in the basket."

Everybody laughed and joked about it and then the subject kind of died down and went away. But not for me. I wondered what I looked like as an infant. I wanted to see my birth weight and footprints too. I felt left out of something that my family members shared amongst themselves. I continued to ask about my baby pictures over the years. I would check family members photo albums whenever we visited. I could never find one and I always wondered what I could have been like as a baby.

Aunt Jane's baby daughter, Cousin Scoop would jokingly say, "girl they ain't take no pictures of you because you were the only pretty baby, dem other mf'er's was ugly!" It was an ongoing joke between us for years.

I began to wonder how it was possible to not snap a single photo of your last baby girl. The thought really broke my heart, but I had to hide that emotion from everyone because I was already labeled as a Problem for being the attention seeking baby. Although my thumb sucking habit and my chair rocking could've attributed to that label.

For years when I was small, I sucked my thumb even though I was afraid that I would end up with bucked teeth. Luckily, an injury resulting from falling out of a tree, put the thumb sucking to an end. The chair rocking was a whole other thing. I would find the most comfortable chair, and rock back and forth for hours at a time. I would just rock my body banging my head against the chair. For some reason I found myself doing it all the time. My siblings would call me weird, tease me, and bully me. I was just different, lighter complected, the light spot on my chin my birthmark, thumb sucking habit, and I've rocked on the chair. I guess that would be a bit of attention seeking unintentionally as a six-year-old to older siblings.

Thing is that the chair rocking went on for years all the way through adulthood. I became known as the rocker to my family. From the inside looking out, I was self-medicating my early anxiety. It had gotten to the point where when we visited family, they would warn Mommy beforehand to keep me off the furniture. I can't really say the rocking was tied to any emotion it became a source of comfort, whether it was happy, or sad, sleepy, energized, or angry I found comfort by rocking on the chair.

I understood messages in music, and I loved it. Never thought I had much of a singing voice, but I would sing along at the drop of a dime even as a kid. Music was a very big deal in my house. Mommy had a record collection that included albums from the carpenters, The Jacksons, Patti LaBelle, Minnie Riperton all the greats from the 60s and 70s. Daddy was a good dancer and singer too. Mommy had some moves, but she wasn't too much of a showoff. I had a natural love for rhythm through poetry and music. Gospel music wasn't allowed in our house, so I learned some of my favorites when I visited my grandmother's house. Daddy's mother was on the usher board of one of the largest Churches in Strawberry Hill.

Chapter 3 This is Us

Strawberry Hill was a housing project perfectly placed in the south side of Baltimore City, which was a fun fact that I discovered later in life. Mommy's oldest sister Jane had a daughter who was also close to me in age. We spent a lot of time together and we shared a cousin bond on a whole different level. Cousin Scoop was from up town, and her parents were gainfully employed. They owned their home in the upper North side of town. We were very close, and their house was my home away from home. Cousin Scoop told me that Mommy was, as she would say with her slick westside draw, "where-fair,-re-sip-e-ent," and Strawberry Hill was the projects. We would laugh so hard about how I didn't know.

I spent the first 16 years of my life on that row of houses. In the 70's & 80's Strawberry Hill Projects was a town of its own. The outside of the rows of houses were made of brown bricks each precisely outlined in white cement and perfect rooftops. I would take my fingers and trace those cement lines between each brick when I was bored, that could be my entertainment for many hours. Sometimes my finger would be white from the cement. Whenever fresh cement was laid, I would carve my name with a stick, and make a footprint in it before it dried so that my memories would last forever. Strawberry hill had one way in and one way out to the entire community. You didn't wanna get lost if you stumbled upon Strawberry Hill, you'd better know somebody who is well known and respected by name. Families lived in Strawberry Hill their entire life. It was like an entire community of relatives really.
Strawberry Hill is tucked away right below busy downtown Baltimore City. In the 70s, starting from the entrance into

strawberry hill you'll be greeted by the famous Music Hall on the right and our personal gas station on the left. As you proceed up the back, at that time dirt road, you'll come across our private apartment homes on the left and then the row homes began on the right. The entire community was full of those lines and rows and rows of brick houses.

In the center of the community there's the community complex and back then, it was known as the multi-purpose center. It served multiple purposes. It's where you would find our doctor, our social services office, the rent office, summer camp, after school programs, community meetings, and even religious gatherings, community events happened there, talent shows, funerals, weddings, anything of a major appearance happened in that same building for years, and the building still stands today.

  Then, Strawberry Hill even had its own shopping center equipped with a grocery store, fast food restaurant, a movie theater, there was the music store, and Barber shops. In addition to the shopping center, there was a stationary goodie bus in three locations throughout the community. The stationary goodie buses provided the sale of goods and snacks if we didn't need to make a trip to the full grocery store. We had a dentist for the community, the same pediatrician for decades, four elementary schools inside that community. Where your row house was located determined which school you attended, they were all fantastic. Strawberry Hill had one middle school located in the middle of the community and everybody from the community attended that school unless you had a high enough grade point average and was given a choice to go to middle school outside of the community. There were a handful of kids who did that.

We had two public transportation buses that came through Strawberry Hill. Just two, and they would take you either downtown or on the West side of town. If you wanted to go to the east side of town, you needed to go to the exit side of the community and board another bus option. The community had two swimming pools, one was indoor, and one was outdoor. The local police station and a major hospital was located inside the community too. Multiple places for worship were situated throughout the community. There was even a real Judge and a politician among the Strawberry Hill residences.
Everything we needed to grow up and a wholesome environment. Every block in between those row houses had its own playground and its own basketball court and its own open field for softball football or flying kites. There's a railroad track that runs along the border of the community. On the other side of the railroad track there was a major highway and other shopping in a different district that wasn't part of the city. It was a county really; we weren't allowed to play over there at all. The rule was simple, don't cross the tracks! Plus, it was very dangerous because trains came through quite often.

  The trains were very loud, so close we would run behind the train and yell at the conductor, "throw a flare, throw a flare," and they would always toss us a few. Sometimes the train would park for hours, then it got interesting. Cause they're in the middle of Strawberry Hill and we're bored so oftentimes robbing the train became the recreational thing to do. Well for many people in my community.

  My house just happens to be on the corner of the row right next to the train track, so the train kept me up a lot of nights. Sometimes though, the rhythm would help me sleep. The sound was one thing, but the smell of that burnt coal and the cloud of smoke that filled my bedroom and lingered in the air, was suffocating. We lived there for so many years growing up, I learned to adapt to that train. Strawberry Hill had one main road that started at the very top of the community and it went all the way to the bottom. That main road was lined with rows and rows of houses and apartments as well. The entire Hill was lined with these beautiful trees from top to bottom. The tree lined streets made the Fall leaves cover the entire hill; it was a beautiful thing to see.

    Back then we did a lot of walking. We walked everywhere, to school, to the shopping center, and places like that. There were a lot of things to also do in the community. Some good, some bad. My row was at the dead end of the hill along with the city dump. The city dump was a huge mountain or landfilled, I guess. There was a dirt road used for driving or walking that cut straight through from the west side of the bottom to the east side of the bottom. The trail was about one mile long, but it led to the other end of Strawberry Hill, where the outdoor swimming pool remains. That shortcut was very scary, because a lot of stray dogs hung out there and a lot of people doing weird things that wasn't always safe. But if you wanted to get to the outdoor swimming pool in a hurry that's your best bet, so my friends and I would always go in a pack.

    As we got older, we explored that landfill and we learned that it was cool. We found so many toys that were thrown out. Different things like roller skates, bicycles, we found out it was a little gold mine. Then for years that's exactly how we treated it. When we needed things to play with, we wanted to build stuff, or even if we had a project that was due for school, we knew just where to go to get our materials, the city dump!

Over the years, the families in Strawberry Hill grew to know and love one another. It was common practice to have community wide cook outs, showers in the fire hydrant, and talent shows. There was a community based marching band, cultural arts programs, and swimming lessons for anyone who was interested. In the summertime we had clean block contest. We'd clean up the whole neighborhood and everybody would help. Bonds were formed that remain intact through this lifetime.

I would often opt to sit outside on my porch with Toby, my dog for hours at a time. The porch was made of cement and the fence was made of thick metal. We painted ours for added appeal. We had a little bit of grass but my favorite thing about that row, was a huge tree in the middle of the block. Everybody would go to that tree almost every single day and we would just be there. The tree offered enough shade to cover everybody's bike in the neighborhood. We sit there on milk crates talk and play for hours every day. Sometimes the trucks will come through and bring free lunch we would gather under the other big tree on the corner. Additionally, we had a goody bus that would come through at night selling snacks for the kids and cigarettes for the grownups. The goodie bus was a huge box truck custom designed by the owner with the same house paint that covered the walls of our house a few years back. The truck would pull up with the horn blowing loudly to signal everyone that he has arrived.

Sometimes the driver would yell out from the window, "Truuuck", and we would all come running. The line would form and when it was your turn to go, you'd step up into the truck. The inside of the truck was completely removed leaving nothing but the driver's seat. Everything in the back of the truck had been replaced to look like a real grocery store. There was a countertop that extended from one side to the next had a piece cut out that served as a passageway to the back of the truck. The driver would go back there and serve customers while the truck was parked. The inventory included chips, cookies, fresh doughnuts, pickles, pickled onions and pickled pigs' feet, candy, toilet paper, cooking oil, butter, cigarettes, top paper, newspapers, and bread. The only place we were allowed to be after the streetlights came on was under the tree. It was the central spot in the neighborhood everybody can look out their window and see who's sitting under that tree.

    I met my lifelong best friend on that row. She lived across the grass from me, in the middle of the row. Ladavious Bug, better known as Ladybug or LB for short. I'm not sure how old we were when we met, but I can't remember a day without her being around. LB was older than me by six months. She was very light completed and had long hair. She was very thin, and her eyes were big and brown like mines. We went to the same elementary school because we lived down the bottom of the Hill. LB was smart like me too. She was the youngest of six in her family, and her siblings were all much older than her. She had two big sisters and three big brothers. Her mom took care of all of them. LB and I instantly bonded and she became my sister for life.

    Daddy had three sisters and two brothers also. One of Daddy's sisters had some daughters. The oldest daughter was Cousin Tricie, and we were only 3 months apart in age. Cousin Tricie had two younger sisters, but I was her best friend because we were so close in age. Cousin

Tricie visited often, and we would spend time together at our grandma's house regularly as we grew up. Grandma, lived in Strawberry Hill too. Daddy's youngest sister lived with her. Her house was at the top of the Hill. Cousin Tricie 's mom lived right across the hallway from Grand mommy and auntie at the top of Strawberry Hill. They lived in an apartment building, but it wasn't part of the rows. They lived in the private section of Strawberry Hill.

    Grand mommy worked as a nurse and Cousin Tricie's mom worked in a factory. Since they had real jobs, they could pay real rent. Since she lived up at the top of Strawberry Hill, Cousin Tricie went to a different elementary school that was located directly across the street from her house. Her elementary school sat adjacent to the community's middle school. It was also much closer to the shopping center than my house on the row at the bottom of the Hill. Back then, the distance between us seemed far greater than it was. Whenever we got together it was like we were in a perfect world. We understood one another without using words. We would laugh at unspoken ideas as if we could hear each other's thoughts.

    Cousin Tricie was light brown complected with full cheeks that looked like perfect bubbles when she smiled. She talked with a lithe because her tongue was fat, she'd say. Cousin Tricie loved food too. She was a little heavy her whole life. I caught up later. Since Cousin Tricie was the oldest of her family, she was mature when it came to situations where she had to choose to do the right thing. When we linked up at grand mommy's house, we were raised like sisters. We attended summer camps together and cultural arts programs. Once we performed the stage play, Cinderella. I played Cinderella and Cousin Tricie played my mean stepmother. We loved to perform on stage. We dressed alike and had countless sleepovers in the years to come. Cousin Tricie was a good girl in my eyes. She would hit me a bible quote from Grand mommy whenever she felt that I needed to be checked. Unlike Cousin Scoop or LB, who's personalities were more like curious risk takers. Nevertheless, over the course of my first decade of life, the foundation was set. The group of us were destined to be friends to the end!

Chapter 4 Sound Foundation

I still remember the first time I saw Daddy in real life. I was very young, from the inside looking out, based on the repeat episodes of "Good Times" when James was away from home working, that was My idea of Daddy. I had only received phone calls and letters before then. One evening we were all in the Living room watching tv.

Mommy was in the kitchen prepping food. The food smelled so good. She was making a huge size Tupperware bowl of potato salad, she seasoned and stored some chicken pieces, doubled a dozen eggs sprinkled with paprika on top, she prepped fish cake patties, and she baked cookies. I begged for samples to the point of annoyance. Mommy explained that she was preparing food for our trip tomorrow. I was confused so I asked what she meant. She told me that tomorrow we were going to visit Daddy. I was so distracted by the food; I quickly went away with the egg before Mommy changed her mind about letting try one. I didn't give any thought to what she said, all I knew was that I was going to have some of that potato salad the next day.

The next morning, Mommy fried the pre seasoned chicken and fish cakes, baked a fresh batch of biscuits, and had everything neatly packed ready to be loaded into our car. Mommy did our hair the night before, so as we unwrapped our does, Roy loaded the car, and we were ready to go. I was super excited about the trip. Roy was too. China and Risha was down for whatever reason, but they weren't as excited. Mommy was excited too. She made sure we looked amazing. We all wore matching leisure suites complete with jackets. Mommy made all of them! Roy washed the car the day before, so it was shiny too. We all piled into our small white four door nineteen seventy something Ford Pinto. Roy rode up front and the girls all in the backseat. The food was in the hatchback. I don't know how long the ride was, but the aromas coming from the hatch had me going bananas the entire time. I rocked and sucked my thumb the whole way. I was interrupted periodically with complaints.

One point I finally invoked the conversation, and I asked, "Where exactly is Daddy?" "Where are going to visit him at?"

The car was silent. I continued rocking in the backseat waiting for the answer. Mommy broke the silence and said, "Daddy is at Camp."

The silence returned. I said, "ok," and that was that. As we rode along, I begin to imagine Camp. I thought it must be so cool to have my Dad work at Camp. He must get paid a lot of money because he is there all the time, and it's hard for Mommy to reach him sometimes. I thought about how Mommy must always wait for him to call her, so he called regularly. I would talk to Daddy about everything. He listened and gave advice. He was always interested in whatever I had to say. He kept me on my toes since I could remember. I was more excited about our visit as we drew closer to Camp. It was my first time seeing him in real life.

When we arrived at Camp, I noticed that it looked like Strawberry Hill except there wasn't any hills, everything was flat. The rows and row of brick houses and buildings were there though. They had the same rhythm. There were groups of houses that each had a private basketball court, and a big grassy field. The coworkers shared a dining hall, and they ate for free, they also shared a gym and recreation hall just like in Strawberry Hill. I wasn't sure what Daddy did to get paid at Camp, but I know Daddy was very important there. I know because when we arrived to visit him, we had to sign in, take a picture, get searched by security, and they even checked our food. After going through the many levels of security, we were allowed inside to wait a long time for Daddy to come out and join us in the waiting room.

Out of nowhere, a security man yelled," Heals out!" I thought, "Wow, my Daddy is famous around here!" Then Daddy appeared. Daddy stood a little over 5 feet 7 inches tall, with a solid fit build, very shiny dark complected, and a small afro. Daddy had a gold tooth on the side of his mouth with the shape of a tear drop on it. He wore huge Cazel eyeglasses, and he was dressed in freshly pressed knacky uniform like James Evans. He had a big bright smile on his face. His stride was excitable, as he dang near hopped and skipped towards us. I had to wait for him to get close enough for me to hug on him, because his security guard was still making sure Daddy was safe. Once Daddy joined us in the waiting room, we all jumped on him hugging and crying tears of joy. Once we all calmed down, we headed outside to the park area for our picnic. Potato salad, here I come!

That day was a special day because a lot of Daddy's coworkers were in the park with their families too. There were picnics all over the field. We were able to visit Daddy regularly over the time that he worked at Camp. Mommy prepared the similar meals each time. I braided Daddy's hair, he taught me how to fly a kite, we ate all that good food, and talked for hours. Daddy had jokes for days and he was witty. He would quiz me on math and spelling. He would coach me on how to watch over Risha. Most importantly, he warned about wooden nickels. Daddy would tell me to never take wooden nickels. I never understood it!

As time passed, I had outgrown most of my custom-made fabrics and I began to share who's ever stuff I could fit. I was the only one who continued to be excited about the visits. The security guards knew me by name because we were there so regularly. I would announce myself as the proud visitor of Mr. Heal. Daddy greeted us with that same big bright smile and excited stride every time. At the end of each visit, Daddy would remind me to never take wooden nickels. I spent so much time trying to figure out exactly what that meant. I would ask Mommy, and she'd say, "That's between you and your Daddy."

By the time I was 7 years old, Daddy began to spend weekends at home with us. I loved having Daddy in our house for a change. He worked so much at Camp; I can't remember him really good at the house before the weekends began. I would be so sad when he had to go. We would sing songs from his favorite group all night long before his long stay away. Earth Wind and Fire would play, and Daddy would be telling me the lyrics to parts that he wanted me to remember. Daddy could sing just like the records. He had a beautiful singing voice and dance moves to match. Looking back over old pictures, I see how much time I spent with Daddy at Camp.

On the weekends, we made up for lost time. We visited family more often, so I got to see cousin Tricie more, and family and friends of Daddy came by to visit us more often too. Mommy would throw special dinner parties on some of those weekends, and invite her cousins and all of Daddy's siblings, and friends.

Daddy had two brothers but only was alive. Daddy's middle brother was killed in Strawberry Hill during the wintertime of the early 1970's, but his three sisters and his one brother would be in attendance. Mommy's two sisters

Judy and Jane would be there as well, along with their cousin Daisy. They would all bring their kids too. It was always a good time when my cousins from uptown came to visit. Mommy's mom was there too, my Grandma Tabby, who refuses to be called anything but Tab by everyone, even her own children. They would all dance, sing, drink, and tell stories and jokes for hours. All the cousins would be running around outside and enjoying the idea of the adult cousins being distracted.

Mommy had the place decorated with balloons and streamers, tables covered, matching plates and bowls for dessert, while outside would be set up with tables, matching folding chairs, and the grill would be going. The speakers would be set up inside and outside of the house with Earth Wind and Fire ringing throughout the rows. The gathering started early in the afternoon and continued until late at night on most weekends.

Sometimes Daddy would get into a big fight with his younger brother, and the party would end abruptly. The fights would be brutal! I would be rooting for Daddy the whole time. The two of them would take to the outside, and then to the vehicles, before you knew it, they'd be racing through the dirt roads of Strawberry Hill waving guns from the car windows completely out of control. Eventually, Mommy stopped hosting the parties all together. The weekend visits began to look different after the parties stopped.

Chapter 5 Best Man for the Job!

Daddy spent time outside more than he used to. He would take me along most of the time.

We would go into a store, and he'd ask, "you want those chips?"

I'd say, "yes sir".

Then he'd say, "get 'em",

So, I'd get 'em.

Then he'd ask, "What are you gonna do wit 'em?"

And I'd say, "eat 'em."

And he'd say, "eat them then".

So, I did. After that, I grabbed snacks everywhere we went. One time, just as we were leaving the store, I'd grabbed another bag of chips. At first, Daddy gave me a silent stare.

Then I looked at him and said, "Risha".
He approved, and we left the store. Daddy visited friends around the city and sometimes things got scary. One time Daddy pulled up on an old friend and he made me wait in the car while they talked. The windows were rolled up so I couldn't hear what they talked about. But whatever it was, it made Daddy real mad. I saw Daddy smack, as he would say, the cowboy poop out of that grown man! The man didn't seem surprised by the smack, he covered the point of impact on his face with his hand, put his head down and walked away.

Daddy aggressively hopped back into the car, reached his hand over to me and said, "hold this."
I grab a fist full of balled up cash.
As Daddy peeled off driving away, he yelled at me, "don't just sit there put that away!"

I quickly stuffed the cash into my front pocket. I kept it there until Daddy remembered that I had it, usually much later in the evening. He would let me keep some for the goodie truck when it came rolling through.
Daddy had a quick temper which caused him to be unpredictable to most people. But not me. I was beginning to know Daddy differently. My role seemed to change from baby girl to right hand man. During the blizzard of 1978, I was eight years old, the city was forced to lock down for days because everything was imploded with heavy snow.

One morning, we were all sitting in the Living room watching the news. The news reporter said the conditions were dangerous and stores were being looted. They advised everyone to stay inside for safety reasons. We needed groceries. The only store available was across the tracks. The snow was over my head and although the trains weren't running, crossing the tracks was still extremely dangerous for anyone. Afterall, that's where Tarzan's Swing was, Strawberry Hill's kids own custom-made death trap!
Daddy grabbed Roy's snow sled and Mommy's Sarah Coventry bag. He emptied the entire kit out from the body sized bag that stood almost my height. He strapped the bag onto the sled with a few bungee cords. Daddy turned on the light, looked at each of us one at a time, without saying a word. We were all silently waiting to hear what he was going to announce. Suddenly, he said, "Cherry, com'on." I hopped right up. I grabbed Roy's snow pants, doubled up my socks, threw on my snow boots, gloves, scarf, hat, and snorkel, ready to go! Toby wanted to go too, but Mommy and the kids was scared that she wouldn't make it.
Mommy said, "y'all be careful", and we were on our way.

The grocery store was located at the top of a tall stretch of road, that was about a mile and a half long. The tracks ran the entire length of that road. Daddy and I had two options. We could've either walked the tracks all the way to the top and then cross over and come out at the back of the store, or we could cross the tracks near our house where the hill was still leveled and then hike up the road until we arrive to the store. We decided to cross at the house. We crossed the track to use that road, which was about a half a mile distance away from our house, the snow was already over my head on the deep parts. We were at the bottom of the hill, hence the deepest part of the accumulated snowfall. Daddy had to put me on his shoulders and carry me. Some of the way, I was able to ride on the sled, and sometimes I even got inside the bag. About two hours had passed before we finally reached the store.

    Other people were there already. People were busying around grabbing what they could. No one was at the register. The floor was wet because people were walking and tracking snow that had melted inside the store. There weren't any shopping carts available, so we dragged the sleigh around the store. Daddy was just tossing anything he could inside that bag. We went straight to the meat department first, and loaded up steaks, chicken, and cans of crab meat. Then we went to the produce section. There we got a bunch of fresh fruits and vegetables. We got snacks and candy, cereal, milk, and juice. I even grabbed two pairs of shoes out the basket on the way out the door one for me and one for Risha. Daddy checked the drawer on the way out. It was already empty. We loaded the bag completely top to bottom with things falling out and hiked back to the house.

    Getting back home was a lot more difficult because now we're lugging groceries. We lost some along the way. I held on to my shoes though. When we got back home it was dark outside, and everybody was so excited that we came back with so much stuff. Mommy fussed at daddy because she knew he didn't pay for anything. She didn't like that. I didn't notice because she got the pots going right away.

The next season Daddy worked a different job. He worked overnight, so during the day he would rest. At his new job he was able to get us free school supplies, we always had tons of notebooks and paper and pencils. When daddy wasn't at work or resting, he was running around with some friends. Unfortunately, daddy fell into some bad ways and started doing some bad things.

Chapter 6 What Just Happened?

Rumors started to spread that daddy was using drugs and that's the reason why he was so short tempered all the time. I always found myself defending Daddy, defending his name. There were lots of rumors in the community. But I never saw Daddy do drugs, so I could never believe that. Yeah, he had mood swings, unexplained missing cash, and he slept more than usual, but daddy worked at night so of course he slept during the day, I'd say.

Then one day LB and I were playing jacks on my porch, because I was punished, and I couldn't get off the porch. Toby was out there with us too. Daddy came home from work. He got out of the car and walked towards the house. We saw him coming but he was taking his time and we thought we had time to throw one more hand before he reached the porch. Toby even slowed him down by running towards him to get a quick show of affection. But by the time daddy reached the porch the jacks were on the hard concrete.

As daddy tried to go into the house, he stepped up onto the porch and he dropped the keys he was carrying. The keys fell right in the middle of the jacks that we had just tossed out on the playing board.
Daddy quickly said, "oh, don't worry let me grab 'em." Then he bent over to pick up the keys. Something fell out of his shirt pocket and onto the porch in the middle of our jacks. It was a small paper packet and a syringe. Daddy quickly picked it up along with his keys, stuck it back in his shirt pocket, and went into the house.

LB and I just stared at one another in shock, we didn't say a word for a few minutes. Before we can get into a decent dialogue about the whole thing, Daddy had returned to the porch. This time he was a completely different person. He was angry. He made me come inside the house and he made LB go away.

Once I got inside, I had to read a few pages of the Encyclopedia Britannica and make a list of twenty new words with their definitions as punishment for inconveniencing him. I spent the next two days in my room. A few days later Daddy overheard me talking on the telephone, explaining to Cousin Tricie why I couldn't come to dance practice. I told her what happened from the beginning and Daddy said that I was telling his business. I ended up getting a beating because I put him in a position to drop his keys and his work on the porch in front of my friend. As time went on daddy was beating me regularly. It seemed that everything I did got on his nerves really bad, because sometimes he would slap me on sight for no reason at all.

He would follow up with saying, "get out my mouth, signifying is worse than testifying!"
I would be furious. Daddy had acquired an addiction to drugs. He wasn't home from Camp for an entire year before he transformed himself into a drug addicted con artist. He boosted from popular department stores and became a completely different person before my very eyes. He would have the whole house filled expensive items with tags still attached on the regular bases. Daddy got us the first everything on the row. We had the first microwave, remote controlled colored tv, and wireless house phone before anyone on our row heard it was coming out. He also got all the latest fashions. Mommy had purses and fancy jewel for every night of the week. They had terrible fights about it. Then they'd make up.

One summer night, Mommy was in the kitchen about to make some salmon and rice. My favorite dish, at the time. She had the fish and onions already in the bowl and she had finished adding the rest of the ingredients. It was really hot that night, so she had the kitchen door opened wide to let the breeze come in while she was cooking. We noticed headlights driving past the front porch, heading towards the train tracks. She looked out the door through the screen and realized it was Daddy parking his pickup truck alongside the train track. The truck was full of all kinds of merchandise. He parked the truck and came inside the house. Mommy blew her top! She screamed at him to move that truck and park it on the street. She said he was doing way too much. Daddy got extremely mad. He began yelling and screaming back at her. He got so mad that he grabbed the bowl of fish mix from the table and hurled it up against the wall in the kitchen. We all jumped up from the living room chairs and ran to our rooms and closed the doors. The fight went on for about an hour.

When the fight was over Daddy was gone and the house was a complete mess. Things were broken and thrown everywhere, and we had no food for dinner that night. Daddy didn't come back until the next day. Sometimes he would return with gifts in hand, and other times he'd return still be on the same bull! He became a monster! I thought he was a real life Jeckle and Hyde. I went from feeling like his best friend to his worst enemy. I wanted nothing more but to get my old Daddy back.

He started getting help for his addiction at the community's drug free program. He would attend meetings and bring home literature about how he could stop using drugs. He never stopped. I would trade anything if Daddy could go back to way he was when he was working at Camp.

I hated that drugs were winning over me. After a while, I became angry too. I didn't stop loving Daddy, but respect for him was fading fast. That was much worst!

Chapter 7 Forbidden Places

Risha and I finished six grades at the same time. After 6th grade graduation, a classmate was throwing a party for all the graduates. Everybody was gonna be there from our class. It was free and it was 4:00 o'clock in the afternoon and it was gonna end probably at 7. LB was gonna be there along with everybody from our class. I wanted to go so bad. There were certain places in Strawberry Hill that we weren't allowed to go near. The graduation party happened to be in one of those forbidden places. My classmate's house was next door to the house where my Daddy hung out at sometimes. I convinced Risha to come along anyway. I told her we would just be a little while and Daddy was at work. We were so cute that day. We were dressed alike. We had on baby blue dresses with matching white tights and white pointy shoes. Our hair was pressed and curled neatly in a mushroom. Risha agreed to come, but with great hesitation. We went, a little late. LB and some other friends were already there. We went inside everybody was surprised and happy that we came. LB had already let everyone know why we were late.

After about 20 minutes or so there's a knock at the door and the music turned down so we all could listen. I heard Daddy say," hey are my girls in there?"
Whoever answered the door said, "yes sir." and I heard Daddy say, "Would you let them know that they need the key to get into the house?"
 They said, "OK."
He came over to me and Risha and said, "hey your dad's outside asking if you have the key, he's not mad or anything."
"I think y'all good, y'all can stay."

"He just asked about the key."
We said, "OK, for real?"
"Yeah", he said.

So, we get to the door, Daddy is standing there. I saw the death stare, clearly on his face. With his teeth clinched together, he told me and Risha to run as fast as we could because we'd better to beat him to the house. He turned around, hopped in the car, and drove away.
I looked at Risha, she looked at me, and we both took off running top speed racing for the house. We had to sprint clean across a glass covered playground, through a fenced basketball court, a poopy grassy field with stray dogs wondering freely about, climb through a hole in the fence to get out of the big grassy field, run up two concrete walkways, and jump up three front steps, to beat that car. And we did! Slippery pointed shoes in all.

I come running in the house top speed, Mommy was at the kitchen sink washing dishes. I was winded, out of breath, had my pretty dress still on, Risha wasn't to the door yet, she was coming though. I was the first one in the house and I was out of breath, and I was yelling at Mommy.
I said, "Mommy Mommy, Daddy told us we could go to the party, and he must have forgot because then he showed up and he just told us to beat him home, but we had permission I know we did…"

Before I could finish explaining, Daddy busted through the door. He heard me tell that lie. He called me out on it.
He yelled, "that's a damn lie!"
I was silent. He then said, "get your lying ass upstairs." Everyone in the neighborhood and throughout the family knew about Daddy's means of harsh punishment, but nobody ever said a word.

I ran up the steps and into my room thinking about how long I had before the beat down. I decided to hide. I was clever, I knew that if I hid under my bed, he would see me immediately as soon as he opened the door. I decided to hide under Risha's bed instead. When I first tried to squeeze under her bed, my hair got caught on a piece of the slack and that was painful. But I kept going. I got all the way up under there as far as I could, and I just sat there for a few minutes balled up. I was thinking of how long it would take before he discovers this is where I'm hiding. Well, I got that answer soon enough.

Daddy came busting in the room he was yelling my name; "Cherry, where you at!?"

I ignored him. Then he started checking. I saw his feet walk over to the closet and open it. I wasn't there, he was so frustrated. He was just about to leave when he realized that I was under that bed.

The next thing I know I saw the mattress fly across the room then I saw the box spring fly across the room and then I saw a big bright light come over me instead of the darkness. The only thing between me and daddy were 3 slacks of wood. Daddy quickly cleared them too. All I could do was ball up and take it. Luckily tossing the furniture helped with some of the energy so this was a quick bout. I stayed balled up and I moved around a lot so Daddy would get tired quick. I got in a few blows and a few kicks, but I let him win. HE was so petty, he kicked Toby on the way out.

It became normal and I found ways to adapt. He would calm down and try to make up with me after a beating by buying me something or taking me outside with him. He continued to teach me about life outside, unintentionally of course. By the time I was ten years old, I felt like the son he never wanted, but I never lost hope of him going back to the Daddy I knew just a few short years earlier.

Chapter 8 Think Differently

Mommy was able to maintain our normal looking family life for the people on the outside. Mommy was extremely private about everything. She hated when Daddy made our house the center of attention. During the years when Daddy was in Camp, Mommy would work all kinds of odd jobs to take care of us. China had to watch or oversee Risha, and I. Roy was allowed to roam freely outside most of the time. The girls usually stayed in the house reading or studying for school.

Mommy was an active member of an organized religious group. We went to Bible study three days out of the week and on days we didn't have Bible study of some sort, we studied independently at home. The organized religion taught me how to read for understanding. Whenever Mommy caught me looking distracted during a meeting, she would silently pinch my skin so hard that my eyes would instantly water. I consistently read through the literature from the meetings, including the Bible, with a highlighter. I made side notes of scriptures that I could find relevant to whatever was going on in my life at the time. By the time I got past the pinch to be quiet stage, I was learning principles of the Bible for myself and my own understanding. By 1st grade I was very good at reading and writing. Before age 6, I understood the scriptures and I began to develop my own personal relationship with God. I wanted God to fix me, so that Mommy and Daddy would love me better and stop fighting all the time.

One day Mommy and Daddy had a terrible fight, a real real bad one. I cried and cried begging for her to just leave Daddy once and for all. I felt like she deserved someone better, someone who treated her better. She always just wanted what was best for us, but Daddy never seemed satisfied.

She explained that the Bible teaches us that we must forgive, and she also explained that it was important for me to talk to God. Mommy told me that God hears our prayers and our thoughts too. She told me that I should always keep my thoughts good, because it was pleasing to God. I was scared when she said that God heard everything even my thoughts and after that conversation, I started thinking differently. I forgave Daddy for being so mean and I prayed for God to forgive me for suggesting that Mommy leave Daddy. Attending the meetings was one of the highlights of my life back then.

At the meetings, there was a question-and-answer part. The microphone would be circulated around the room for anyone who wanted to share a thought. I couldn't wait for my turn. I wanted to say, "In harmony." so bad. That was the jargon used if, when the microphone got to you, and someone had already shared your exact thought, instead of repeating it, you'd just say, "In harmony". I thought it was such a cool gesture So, I kept my hand raised a lot. Before the meetings. we had to prepare. We prepared by pre reading all the literature and making notes as to what we'd say if got called on. We practiced how we were going to answer each question if we were asked. I was always ready.

The congregation members sung together as an entire congregation, everybody had songbooks with all the words to all the songs. There wasn't a choir. They had extra bibles for people who didn't bring their own. The organization had conventions too. They were a big deal. Mommy would do her normal cooking feast and pack up for the road trip. We usually would bring along a random friend who needed a ride. The convention was usually about an hour drive away from the house maybe longer. The grounds were beautifully landscaped. There were tons of multicolored flowers and beautiful trees, and a long brick driveway that led up to a huge, beautiful building surrounded by more beautiful landscaping.

    To me, the conventions were equivalent to the setting of, The Candy Man. I could almost hear Sammy Davis Jr singing Candyman..." Who can take the sunrise, sprinkle it with dew, cover it with chocolate, add a miracle or two...?" The inside of the building was immaculately decorated. There was a waterfall as soon as you walked inside, and you could see the pool used for baptisms off to the side. The dining hall was huge, and it had beautiful drapes hanging that covered all the walls. I could smell the food from the lobby. In the morning breakfast included fresh cut fruit, hot or cold cereals, eggs cooked however preferred, choices of meats, choices of bread like fresh baked biscuits waffles or toast, and a juice bar along with a coffee bar with all the fixings. The lunch menu changed daily from one delicious day to the next. I can't describe the different varieties of foods and desserts I tried that weekend, but I learned about a Cornish hen for the first time at the convention. Mommy would have us dressed in our best attire for those two days. The meetings ran from sunup to sundown over two days. At the conventions, new congregation members would get baptized. The congregation would also put on an assembly portraying one of the books from the Bible. They would have costume, makeup, and live music, it was the best thing ever like watching a live Broadway show.

    Daddy would attend the conventions and special meetings if he was around at the time. But most of the time he heard about the conventions and meetings from me.

Daddy would visit the club sometimes too. The brothers at the club hated to see him coming. Daddy didn't care about the rules at the club. He walked in there and comfortably sat and behaved however he felt in that moment. Sometimes he might talk too loudly, or move around too much in his seat, he might even step outside and smoke a cigarette. But nobody would dare to check him. Nobody.

    Mommy never missed a meeting. Even on school nights we had to attend the meeting, and we stayed for the full service all the way to the end of the last song. We would rush home get ready for school the next day.

Mommy worked a lot of jobs and she had so many different skills and hobbies. She could sew, make clothes, do hair, clean houses, cook and she could dress nice. When things needed to be done, she expected us to hop to it.

She'd say, "don't be sitting there like a bump on the log you better move!"

    She had us washing clothes, hanging clothes, folding clothes, cooking dinner, cleaning the house, reading books, learning to drive, you name it we were doing it. Me and my sisters had to tend to the garden, help at the grocery store, and anything else that girls were supposed to do. Mommy had a mindset where even when Daddy was away at prison, he oversaw the house. And everything had to be cleared by Daddy. Daddy knew all about the club we were attending to practice our organized religion. He didn't object, but he never got fully invested like Mommy. They were complete opposites when it came to that.

Chapter 9 Wildflower

After school and on weekends, Mommy had to bring me with her to her jobs. She was cleaning houses for rich people who lived in affluent neighborhoods. I loved going to work with Mommy. I looked forward to the lunch! After a while, Mommy changed jobs and I couldn't come to work with her as often.

My idled mind had me all over the place. I got good at a variety of things. Like spelling, cutting grass, writing, braiding hair, reading, and dancing. As I got a little older, Mommy was bothered about some of my behaviors and hobbies. Spending time with Daddy enabled me to see outside. I was too interested in outside. I wanted to spend time with LB and other kids from the rows. Mommy would say, "Bad association spoils useful habits." I thought to myself, there's so much to do in Strawberry Hill if I could just get off the porch! I began to explore.

When Daddy was away at Camp, and Mommy was busy with work, I would take full advantage of the freedom. LB and I would be all over Strawberry Hill having the time of our lives. We secretly joined girl scouts, the marching band, and a softball team, with no adult permission! I was sneaking out of the house since I was 7 years old, quite regularly. We would venture off to the top of the Hill to visit Cousin Tricie, and we would visit some of the other school grounds around the Hill. We would buy snacks and sodas all day, I always had a little money in my pocket. On occasions where I didn't get back to the house before Mommy, she would do exactly what Daddy would do if he was there. Beat me.

Mommy's beatings were worse because she hurt my body and my feelings at the same time. I empathized when her and Daddy had disagreements, but now she's beating me too. There were times when the two of them joined forces. She would say, "you're always going to be a problem". I couldn't understand how though. I wanted to please her as much as I wanted to please Daddy, maybe even more so. I was so curious about everything; I didn't feel like I belonged. I guess I started to internalize being a problem like Mommy said. I found hobbies to keep me busy. I was cutting grass, braiding hair, and running errands for money around the neighborhood with a list of clients at 8 years old. Mommy was annoyed if I wasn't at house in time to go to the meeting. Missing a meeting was a guaranteed beating. Sometimes, I'd get left all together and got dealt with later. I continued to rock on the chairs when I was upset or bored, and I continued to get beatings for rocking on the chair, but after a while, it didn't matter to me. I started writing poetry and journaling. I learned to do that when I needed to express myself because I didn't have an audience. We didn't talk in the house much. We just survived.

    I had begun to develop curves on my body. My hips were rounding, and I was growing boobs a little. I started noticing that my deodorant struggled at the end of most days. I even had a slight case of acne. I had outgrown clothes in the girl's section of Epstein's and it was hard for Mommy to find things that fit me. China and Risha never had that problem because they remained a normal size. Mommy had to alter all my clothes. I got hand me downs from bigger people, but there was still a problem. The garments were oftentimes out of my age range for appropriateness. I was the youngest, but I had to dress like the oldest. I could fit all of Roy's clothes. I had to put a bend in the length or tuck the bottoms down in my shoes for a nicer fit. I could fit some of China's tops, but I dare not touch any of her belongings! Mommy had lots of skirts and blouses that I would sneak and wear to school when I could get away with it.

One day I needed some clean underwear so that I could get dressed for outside. Mommy hadn't gotten to the laundry yet, so I borrowed a black pair from her underwear drawer. The next day, Mommy was getting dressed and she needed that pair of black underwear. She discovered what I did and confronted me. I paid dearly! On top of that, the whole thing was overheard through the walls. The house next door was where Deserae lived. Her bedroom closet attached to mines, so every single word and movement was witnessed by her and LB, who just happened to be hanging out there at the same time! The next day when I up with LB, the first thing she yelled was, "I WANT MY BLACK UNDERWEAR!" and we both burst out laughing. After a while we continued with our day. Mommy would always catch me and LB whispering and laughing to ourselves. She felt that we were up to no good. Most often, we were. It had gotten to the point where I tried to negotiate my consequences. I would ask can Mommy beat me this time? or Can I take the beating instead of the days? I was no longer affected by the treatment I received in the house; overtime it helped me grow.

When I ran away from home for the first time, I wrote a poem that read,
"Here I leave this penny, one of great concern. One day I will need it, and that's when I'll return."

I taped a penny to a sheet of notebook paper and placed it neatly on my pillow. I packed a few shirts, some shorts, and snacks and left the house. I went straight across the grass to LB's house. LB let me in, and we talked about next steps. LB wanted to run away too but her mom was home, and she couldn't sneak out. We sat there plotting on how we could make it happen. This was bigger than the times when we hid in her house, while staking out mines looking for signs that Daddy was sleeping so we can hook school. LB whipped out her note pad and we begin to strategize losing all tracks of time. It didn't take long for Mommy to come checking for me. After I returned to the house and got my beating, my siblings teased me and laughed about my poem. Roy said you sure needed that penny quick. They all laughed about that poem for many years ahead!

From the inside looking out, I felt even more distant in the house ever since that first time I ran away. I begin to do what Mommy warned me about often, I begun to stray away from the teachings of our organized religion. I had questions that I didn't get answers to. I still didn't understand how saying a pledge in school, celebrating my birthday, or even accepting a present was not allowed. Mommy was annoyed whenever I questioned her about some of the practices based off the teachings from our organized religious group. It didn't make sense to me because what I saw did not match what I was experiencing in my house.

I felt that I was missing a big piece of the picture. Mommy had a scripture for every question. I was taught that it is a show of disrespect to question my parents about any teachings they gave me. I tried to make sense of things for myself. At that time, I was maturing and quickly approaching puberty. Mommy became more of a supervisor regarding her dealings with me. Sometimes, she too had moments where her rage won. We didn't attend family functions because most of the time they had a holiday theme. Mommy only allowed us to spend time with people from the club.

Daddy felt that his family needed to be a part of our lives, so we continued to associate with close family only. Cousin Tricie and her sisters were allowed to sleepover at our house on occasions.

This evening, Mommy cooked fried chicken, rice with gravy, and string beans. She baked a cake and put s shaped designs in the icing. We loved rice and gravy. Mommy cooked it with almost every meal. At dinner time, we all gathered at the large dinner table, Mommy says the grace, and we eat.

Cousin Tricie and I had inside jokes between only us, so eye contact would invoke uncontrollable laughter without warning. Daddy was sitting there enjoying his meal. Cousin Tricie and I both waiting for him to flip for no reason. Every little thing was just so funny to us because we're secretly anticipating an eruption at any time. Risha dropped her fork, but that didn't do it. Roy cleared his throat, and that didn't do it either. Cousin Tricie and I snickered out loud a little this time, and that did it!

We didn't realize that everyone sitting at the table were nervously on edge and we were the only two who found it funny. Mommy got so angry at us for our foolishness, she started fussing about it. Cousin Tricie was so caught off guard that she began to choke on her rice! Within seconds, the kitchen was in an uproar! Mommy rushed over to save Cousin Tricie's life while fussing the whole time, Daddy stood up ready to spring into action, China slid her plate further away from Cousin Tricie while rolling her eyes, Roy folded his arms and stood next to Daddy, Risha started crying, and I could not control my laughter.

By the time we finished ruining dinner, Mommy was handing out slaps to anyone within reach. Cousin Tricie and I had to clean the kitchen and when she went home real early the next morning, we didn't have sleepovers again for a long time. But I still saw Cousin Tricie regularly because Mommy had to leave me with Grand mommy when she couldn't leave me at the house with China and Risha anymore.

Chapter 10 I know that was God

I didn't listen good enough for China to watch me after a while. The last time China was in charge, I escaped and ventured off with LB and her cousin Nikki, who was also a girl scout. It was wintertime and we needed something to do. We were dressed for the great outdoors. I had on my big blue snorkel coat, extra socks on my hands and feet, and my hat and scarf. The three of us decided to go ice skating on the frozen lake that surrounded the dump. Most of the snow had melted away but we could find small patches here and there. We'd pause along the way to toss a few snowballs. The frozen lake looked like a real ice-skating ring. Small green bushes lined the edges all the way around it. We checked for cracks on the ice before we skated. We only pretended to have on real skates, were all wearing snow boots. We all slid onto the sheet of ice slowly one at a time. When we felt secure, we began going around the ring. We went around a few times and then I spotted a small pile of snow tucked away beneath a few of the bushes. Before LB or her cousin could say anything, I went charging towards it.

I jumped right in thinking I was going end up on my feet standing on the bush at best. However, when I jumped in, I kept going! I jumped right through the ice! I was trapped under the frozen lake. It happened so fast. I was trapped under the sheet of ice trying to find the same hole that I came through, but I had drifted away from it. I began to panic and pray. I went towards some shadows and light coming from over my head and then I saw a green hose hanging down. It was the opening. LB and her cousin Nikki had found a piece of broken water hose in the dump, stuck in into the hole and yelled for me to grab it and to hold on to it real tight. I did. They pulled me out of that lake to safety. LB had tears in her eyes. She grabbed my arms, instructed her cousin Nikki to grab my feet, and they carried me all the way to the house. I was so cold I thought my blood had turned into ice.

When we got to my house, China was in the kitchen washing dishes. LB opened the front door, and they stepped inside still struggling to carry me. LB and her Nikki slowly placed me down onto the kitchen floor. China never stepped away from the sink.
She just turned her head my way, looked us over, and said, "You're gonna get it Dummy!"

LB and Nikki left before they got accused of being my, "company while Mommy wasn't home."
China told Mommy about how I got out without her knowing and how I wouldn't listen to her when she told me to do things.

Mommy gave me a beating with an extension cord for that. She was infamous for grabbing whatever was in reach to be her weapon of choice. Over the years I had gotten hit with all sorts of things like the bristle side of a hairbrush, combs, wire hangers, shoes, slippers, wooden paddle, cooking utensils, leather belts, clothesline rope, tree branches and curtain rods. Just to name a few. Daddy started calling me Tough Tony.

By 9 years old, I slowly straying away from Mommy's ideals, and I was in full discovery mode. I was missing meetings on purpose by then. I would get to the house late from school or I would play so hard that I needed a whole bath and a new hairdo before I could go anywhere. Mommy had sort of threw in the towel with me by then and left my dealings up to Daddy. I was a true tomboy and I stayed busy with outside stuff. Outside, I learned how to dance, write poems, play games, and discover stuff outside of the organized religious group that I was still a part of. I hung out more with Daddy and I was his personal runner when he needed cigarettes from the bus. I would go get them for him. Daddy smoked cigarettes and we all hated it, especially me. The smell of the old ashes made me sick! I thought it was the most disgusting thing ever. However, the smell of Daddy's freshly lit cigarette wasn't that bad. Mommy didn't like me buying cigarettes from the bus for Daddy. She didn't think it was appropriate for me to even be near cigarettes. Daddy knew that I could handle the task. Daddy thought that I could handle any task, just as I thought of him. This caused more tension between Mommy and me. She would say I was always going to be a "problem".

    One day I got to the house late and nobody was there. I was locked out and it was getting dark outside. I waited at LB's house until her mom said I had to go because it was a school night. I went over to my house and sat down on the wooden porch chair. I was cold, hungry, and tired. The streetlights were on and still nobody came. I waited and waited because I had no other options but to wait. Finally, Mommy and my siblings arrived. Mommy parked the car and they all hopped out. Instead of heading to the house, they all went to the trunk of the car. Mommy opened it and they started pulling out large shopping bags. When they approached the house and saw me sitting there, everyone was quiet until we got inside of the house. Once inside, I was able to see the bags. They had been to dinner and shopping without me. They had left over food from the restaurant and drink cups. Risha didn't bring me anything. Nobody brought me anything.

They had new outfits for school and Risha said, "ain't nothing fit you in there anyway." Mommy looked at me and said, "you should have been here."
I was crushed. That was far worse than any beating or punishment that I had ever got.

Mommy realized that it was effective, so excluding me from things became a common practice at the house. Resentment had accumulated inside of me. I made a few more attempts at running away, but I could never get far. I wanted to go to Camp, like Daddy, to get away. Mommy was angry with me all the time. I was a big disappointment to her. I couldn't do anything right!

In 3rd grade, Risha and I were in the same class. That was a tuff schoolyear for both of us. We were getting bullied every day, me for my birthmark and Risha for her eye patch. We got bullied for going to the club all the time too. I had to protect Risha from the bullies when things went too far. Mommy said sticks and stones may break your bones, but names will never hurt you. Names did hurt though, and I didn't like pain! Me and LB got into so many fights with random kids before, during and after school, Mommy thought that I was the bully.

Although Risha was older than me, I was the one who had the accountability on behalf of both of us. Mommy didn't like how LB seemed to be more of a sister to me than Risha. That year, I got straight A's on my report card. Risha failed and was required to repeat 3rd grade. When Mommy and Daddy got the news, I got the worse beating ever! They were furious as to how and why I got straight A's, and Risha missed the mark, while we were in the same class. They felt that I must have been ignoring her when she needed help and trying to get involved with worldly things instead. From the inside looking out, I knew for sure that something in my house was terribly wrong! After that, I didn't want to do well in school anymore, but I couldn't do bad in school either. I became quiet in my dealings with the house. I continued to do well in school, but I scaled back a little bit. I started getting at least one or two Bs on my report cards to keep the peace. I had accepted the label of black sheep of the family.

Chapter 11 My Daddy, My Hero

From the inside looking out, I learned back in preschool that being affiliated with an organized religious group, would require me to behave differently in class from my peers. I was not allowed to stand and say the Pledge of Allegiance to the flag. Mommy taught us that in our organized religion the flag represented a false God and to pledge allegiance to it would be praising a false God. So, we weren't allowed to do the pledge all through school. A lot of the kids from my row attended the same school, and when birthday celebrations were held in class, I had to be excused from participating. Some of my classmates would become offended, assuming that I was receiving special treatment. Preschool conflicts are real!

I started school at 3 years old. Preschool was little red building situated right on the parking lot of the elementary school that I would be attending later all the way through 5th grade. The little red school gave me the first opportunity to meet other children in and around my neighborhood, and to see what real school was like. It wasn't until second grade that I started to see things differently. By that time, I was reading and writing fluently and making sense of things. I found myself excluded from things as simple as never being chosen to hold the flag. I was restricted from participating in any activity involving holiday themes. I felt punished for existing. My peers noticed, so I had to compensate by excelling in academics. I entered kindergarten understanding basic arithmetic, reading, and writing.

From the inside looking out, it was how I first learned the truth about Daddy. One day while at free time, me and some other kids were all gathered under a tree talking. I was talking about Daddy's amazing job at Camp and how important he was. I was telling my friends about the awesome picnics we had. We were all just talking and laughing and having a good time. Then this kid from a different block of rows, says the unthinkable.

He said, "girl, you're dumb as hell, your Daddy ain't in nobody's Camp!"

"That Ninja is locked up!"

I denied it, I said, "what are you talking about?" "My Daddy is at Camp, I go see him all the time he's not locked up."

The kid said, "yes, he is, because my Big Brother is over there with him, and he rec with your Daddy every day."

I was stunned and in disbelief. I wanted him to be making it all of that up. I went home, and I told Mommy what had happened. I asked her was it true. Mommy told me, to stay in a child's place, that was not my business. The next visit to Camp, I told Daddy what my friend at school had said. Daddy didn't confirm or deny that Camp was really prison. He said that the little boy was just trying to be fresh with me, not to let him blow in my ear and make my drawers fall down. He warned me to stay away from him at all costs! And so, I did.

Later, I found out that that kid was telling the truth. Daddy really was in prison all those years and I didn't know. Finding that out made me feel different about everybody. I thought, why would they keep that from me? How could they? I thought finally, that's it!

From the inside looking out, he was like a stranger to me; I didn't know who this man was. I wondered what he did to get in jail. I felt different going to visit him at Camp. I was still in shock after I learned that Daddy's security team was really corrections officers, and the park was a prison yard, and the coworkers were all locked up too! Mommy got annoyed every time I asked about it, she didn't like having to explain herself or him to me. Roy and China seemed to have already known that Camp was really prison, they were in on it too. I couldn't help but wonder who else knew that Daddy was a criminal.

By fourth grade, Daddy was home from prison for longer periods of time. Often, he would be stretched out sleep on the couch in the mornings when I'd be off to school. I noticed how he would be partially responsive because he was so tired. I needed change for school and when I'd ask him, he would always signal me to grab a few coins that was laying around the contents of his pockets. Daddy would empty his pockets out and leave a pile of stuff next to him as he slept. The pile could include change, bills, cigarettes, rolling paper, lighters, lottery tickets, gum, rubber bands, knives, and dice. I would usually grab enough change for snacks throughout the day. Daddy never questioned me about the amount of money or what I used it for.

I was entering my rebellious stage, and I began to experiment with the things that Daddy found so enjoyable. First up, smoking. One day when I was collecting my change for school, I noticed that Daddy's cigarettes were spilled out onto the floor. I decided to take one. I was excited to add to the collection and fit in with LB's other friends who were already bringing cigarettes to school every day. As time went on, I was taking a few of Daddy's smokes every day.

LB and I cut school one day and we planned to go check out a movie. We hid out in LB's house until we thought the coast was clear before we headed out to the bus stop. We both stole free passes from our older siblings who attended high schools that provided them with free public transportation. The bus stops were on just about every main block throughout Strawberry Hill. We strategically walked to the bus stop that was a bit off the main road just in case we were spotted by members of The Club who would be on the corners pushing their magazines. When we arrived at the bus stop, we waited and planned how we would survive the consequences if we got caught. It got stressful, so we lit up. At first, we coached one another on the correct way to inhale the smoke. The taste was absolutely disgusting! It burned a little and I choked after the first few drags. It wasn't until the entire cigarette was gone the effects kicked in from out of nowhere. At ten years old, we're standing on the bus stop during school hours, smoking cigarettes and suddenly, the most uncontrollable laughter showed up. We were almost on the ground laughing when we noticed the enormous blinding shine from the front grill of Daddy's pick-up truck coming over the horizon of the hill.

  For a split second, I froze hoping to match the huge tree that marked the spot. My nerves wouldn't allow the stillness. I broke! I took off running! I ran down the block and circled around the random block long row of brick houses that lined the street. After running the entire perimeter of the row, I paused at the top and peeked around the corner with Daddy and LB still at the tree. My heart went out to her, but not enough for me to surrender. I stayed tucked. I waited for Daddy to make his next move. To my surprise, he drove away.
I yelled to LB, "where'd he go?"
She said, "he's gone."

I came out of hiding and joined LB on the bus stop again. Daddy told her to let me know that he saw me and to have fun. We both knew what that meant. Why would I initiate my punishment early? I figured that I may as well get all my rocks off while the opportunity was clearly presenting itself. Without hesitation, we hopped on the bus. We flashed our passes and took a seat still rolling with laughter about how fast I got outta there!

The bus was empty because the morning rush was over, and everyone was in school or at work. We arrived downtown and proceeded straight to Lessthanten Market for lunch. We got fried chicken necks and gizzards with hot sauce. We ran into some other kids who were cutting school too and they had more cigarettes. We all went to the movies and had the best time ever. When the after-school time came, we all hustled back to Strawberry Hill and got off the bus at the store so that we could take the scenic route home and blend in with the kids who really attended school that day.

Chapter 12 Divine Intervention

Daddy worked second shift and he would get home from work pass midnight on most evenings. I made sure Daddy was well off to work before I made my way to the house. In my mind, I planned to have all my chores done, my completed homework laid out on the kitchen table, and I wanted to be very sleep when Daddy arrived home from work. I prayed real real hard! It was at these times, I wished Daddy was high, because he would likely be chill and relaxed. He might even find the whole thing funny. I worried like crazy on my best behavior all evening. I even prepared for bible study that wasn't until the next night. It got later and later so I thought Daddy must have made a pit stop and that was good news. I tried my best to fall asleep, but I couldn't. That's thing about the wooden nickels, you just never know what to expect. I couldn't be more wrong about Daddy's mood.

He came home high at about 2 AM. Daddy made his abrupt entrance into the house. He slammed the door and stormed through the house cussing and tossing things around. I squeezed my eyes shut tight and bawled my body up real tight under my covers. I didn't want to breathe. Then the moment came.

I was terrified when Daddy yelled, "CHERRY! GET YOUR MONKEY ASS DOWN HERE NOW!"
I literally could not get downstairs fast enough, because before my feet hit the floor, Daddy was busting through the bedroom door. He flicked the light switch on with so much force, a spark whipped out. He grabbed me by the collar of my pj's so quick, I didn't realize I was already tossed across the room. He was like a mad man! He cussed me out for a while and when he didn't get the reaction he needed,

Daddy snatched off his thick leather work belt, doubled it up, and commenced to whip the cowboy poop out of me! Shortly after, I linked up with LB for morning walk to school. On the way, we compared bruises. We both had got it bad! We didn't mention that part to anyone, ever! Instead, we became blood sisters. We both made a small cut on our fingers and mashed them together. From the inside looking out, we were real sisters! We continued with our shenanigans and learned to navigate around our lives at home. We accepted the fact that consequences will come with our choices.

  The biggest difference between Mommy and Daddy when it came to consequences was while Mommy would grab any object, Daddy would stick to the leather belt. The beatings would last for a few minutes and Daddy would quickly wear himself out. After so many, I became immune.

  Mommy on the other hand, would talk through the whole thing and she never got tired! I started to believe; I was getting the revenge she couldn't give Daddy. Mommy beating me was worse than Daddy beating her. She had those sharp little fingers and a grip like no other! I remember being called "the Problem" no matter what the situation was. Mommy made me understand that I was not special just because I was light skinned.

  I never thought that my complexion was light. In fact, my birthmark was the only light spot on me. Mommy could never explain to me what it symbolized. I never stopped asking her about it. I asked so many questions about myself, I got a few beatings for bothering her. I wanted to know who I took after in my family. I wondered if anyone else had my birthmark too. That's when Mommy got irritated most. She would always tell me that I look like everybody.

    I was getting older and by ten, I officially entered puberty! I had the worst tummy ache ever. I felt heavier than normal. My thighs plumped up and they stayed that way. My butt sat up like it was at full attention. I rocked on the chair often and I developed a tiny waist. I struggled to find clothes that fit. I was ashamed of my body because I got teased a lot. Risha was the worst. She would call me fat and other mean names. Roy and China would encourage her to challenge me because she was older, and I should listen to her. They were right and every time we got into our normal sibling rivalry behavior, Mommy would step in and get ME together!

    The bickering would usually end with me sent to bed early even when I was too old to still be getting sent to bed. I didn't know then that I needed to feel connected to them but instead, I was rejected on many levels. I didn't have a voice and I could never be seen. Especially when Daddy was away at prison. It was those times when our home life was different.

    When Daddy was away for months at a time, Mommy had to raise all of us alone. She relied heavily on her friends who she fellowshipped with. She had routines in place, and she ran a tight ship! My siblings and I had very clear expectations and we were held accountable. Mommy began college when I was entering middle school. Daddy continued to struggle with the law and his drug addiction. The fights were consistent and as my siblings and I got older, we gained our own ideas about our situation. I became more and more interested in spending time at Cousin Scoop's house, because I had a sense of freedom there. I could talk, write, go roller skating, or just hang outside in the neighborhood with Cousin Scoop's friends. I didn't feel like I was walking on eggshells. My opinion mattered there. Mommy considered that to be bad association because we didn't practice that type of freedom in our home. She warned me that God didn't favor bad association because it was worldly. I felt like Mommy was ashamed of me for existing, and I needed to be perfect to be loved by her. I was convinced that was the reason why she never talked about love. From the inside looking out, she was not practicing what she was teaching.

 I was about twelve years old when Daddy met his match. One Saturday morning, we loaded up the car with a bunch of clothes and other collectables that Mommy was going to sell at the local flee market. It was a hobby that her, Tab, her big sister Jane, and her younger sister Judy all loved to do. They all met at the rented spot and set up shop for the day. I would come along because all my cousins would usually be there too, and we would enjoy our time together for the whole day. Cousin Scoop and I had already planned for me to leave with them when it was time to go. It was summertime, school was out, and we wanted to go skating later that evening, so we earned money by helping with the sales for most of that day. Mommy said that I could go, and Aunt Jane had no issues. At the end of the day, we finished cleaning up our spot, and it was time leave. The parking lot was halfway emptied out. I got in Aunt Jane's van and sat patiently waiting for everyone else to finish up.

 All the sudden, Daddy appeared from out of nowhere. He slung Aunt Jane's sliding van door opened, grabbed the entire collar of my shirt breaking my skin with his fingernails, snatched me out of the seat and slammed my body onto the ground. I looked up from the ground and my face was met with his boot. He stomped and stomped away at me until Aunt Jane stepped in. She jumped on his back and punched away at his face from behind. He shook her from him, and they were squared up, eye to eye. I knew we were about to finally whip Daddy's ass! My face was leaking blood, and tears were rolling down my face, but I stood to my feet and took my place beside my Auntie. Mommy never said a word and she never moved from her neutral spot. Daddy was beyond furious.

Auntie told him, "Ninja, I will cut your Mutha F'n head off and watch it roll down that cliff if you think about putting your hands on my niece again!"

Daddy was on go! He yelled, "That's my child!" "She do what the f*ck I say!"

He charged at her. He didn't think about all her kids and all the other family members standing around. Everybody jumped on him, including China and Risha! Auntie's oldest daughter was nine months pregnant at the brawl. She put in so much work on Daddy, she delivered her baby later that night. Daddy went back to jail, and I spent a few weeks at Cousin Scoop's house. Cousin Scoop shadowed boxed all night long recalling the events of the fight. She said, "We need to do that again!" We laughed ourselves to sleep.

Book 2
Pupa & Chrysalis

Chapter 13 Middle School

After being on punishment over most of the summer break, I was looking forward to returning to school. Risha and I were heading to middle school. Kids from all four of the elementary schools in Strawberry Hill were going to be attending the same school building at the same time. We were going to among kids from up the Hill and throughout the middle. I was looking forward to the middle school lunch menu Roy and China bragged about the whole time they attended the big school. Cousin Tricie and LB was going to attend the same middle school too. China would be there for last year of middle school as well. Roy was already off to High School.

Over the summer, I spent my time on punishment. Mommy would only allow me to go outside to maintain my grass cutting gigs around my immediate rows. I entertained myself by reading the encyclopedia and writing lyrics in my room most days. I'd help Roy practice his wrestling and boxing moves. He played on teams in high school. That was long summer.

It's a good thing I did! On my big first day of middle school, I had on my best fitting new school jeans that I could not wait to wear because they didn't gather up when my thighs rubbed together, and my bright white ruffled collar blouse, and some fresh pumpkin seeds with cute little puppy print shoes on my feet. Me, LB, and Cousin Tricie were all in the same class. To add to the group, Shante' moved to our row right before we summer started and we were all friends. We all sat at the same group of desks in the back corner of the classroom so that we could see everyone else. We had something for everybody. We saw some new faces and we made some new friends. The first half of the school day was going great. Then it was time to transition into lunchtime.

The cafeteria was located on the first floor of the school building and my classroom was on the third floor of the building. Two separate stairwells led to the first floor of the huge school building. When the bell rung, we all made our way to the middle stairwell because it was the closest one to our classroom. All the kids crowded the hallways heading towards the stairwells. As we walked in the fast-moving crowd, a group of boys walked behind us.

I could hear them giggling and talking about something being big and then I heard one of them say, "I bet it jiggles."

They all continued laughing and walking behind us.

As we entered the stairwell, they got closer to us, like we were on a crowed elevator. I looked back and this one boy had the silliest grin on his face, I didn't say a word. I turned back around and took another step forward with the crowd. I felt something squeeze my but!

I turned around again, this time that same boy said, "It does", to his friends.

Before anyone could say anything, I clinched my fist, drew it back, and released a haymaker that I know he must remember to this day! The crowd opened up, I turned around and we continued our brisk walk to the cafeteria.

As we crossed the entrance into the cafeteria, we spotted our assigned table and headed that way. I could hear some commotion from behind us.

Then LB calmly said, "Yo, he's coming".

I turned around and I saw the boy storming my way. He had his fist clinched, shoulders tightened up, and he was breathing hard. I remained calm, knowing that this was about to be my moment, cause boy, I been needing to whip somebody's ass for a very long time! Let's Go!

As he approached me, he was yelling at me, "You hit me in my face, you fat Bitch!"

He was already winded by the time he got close to me. I never said a word, I let him get arms reach away from me, just like Roy showed me. I didn't give him a chance to raise his fist before I hit him with a right -left - right to his chin. It went, blip, blip, blip real fast. He didn't know what was going on. I quickly switched to wrestling mode. I grabbed him up and slammed his whole body into one of the large garbage cans that the school had scattered around the cafeteria.

    I got sent to the principal's office. I explained what happened, but they still insisted on calling my house. I knew Daddy would be angry because he would usually sleep while we were in school. When Daddy got the call, he hadn't been to sleep yet but he was busy doing something. He told the principal to put me on the phone. I took the phone and put it to my ear.

I said, "Hey Daddy."

He said," Hey Daddy shit! What happened!?"

I told him that a little boy touched my but and I banged him in his face, and he got mad and wanted to fight.

Without hesitation, Daddy yelled, "Did you put his punk ass down!?"

I said, "Yes sir."

Daddy proudly yelled, "That's my girl!"

I looked up at the principal and she had a confused look on her face. She overheard Daddy's response. I knew it because she curled her lip in the corner, raised her eyebrow, and put a star beside my name that was written down on her big desk calendar. Daddy had already hung up his end of the phone. I sat there with the phone still up to my ear. The principal stared at me.

I slowly handed the phone over to her and said, "He said, 'okay'."

I returned to my class feeling assured that Daddy was good with my choice to handle the situation like he had always advised me. All the kids were still excited about the fight they saw. The boy was sent home because he started it. Everyone said that I beat him up bad. After that, our whole squad became popular at school. Risha and I didn't get bullied anymore. I maintained my status of Tomboy all through middle school.

Most of the girls in middle school, were into boys, but not me. I wanted to write, make music, and drive. Before finishing middle school, three girls from my class had kids. A few more of them had secret pregnancies and had abortions. The most important goal through middle school was programmed into my brain from day one.

Mommy in one ear would say, "bad association spoils useful habits."

That meant, stay away from people who could have a bad influence on me.

Daddy in my other ear would say, "Don't ever let a ninja blow in your ear and make your drawers fall down."

I got the message loud and clear from both! I stayed busy with the afterschool programs when I wasn't on punishment. In middle school I was exposed to so much, that my curiosity about things often got the best of me. I took a lot of risks. I attracted a lot of attention with making jokes all day. I didn't want to be labeled as a mean girl. I made people laugh and I talked loudly. I was every teacher's worst student.

One day I went too far in my French class. My teacher, Ms Stooper AKA Madaam Stoo-pear, had enough of it one day. She was in the hallway during transitions, as my class entered her room for our French lesson. My clique and I decided that it would be funny to erase the work from the chalkboard while she was in the hallway on duty. We did! When she came into the classroom, everyone was staring at her instead of working, waiting to see her reaction.

When she cussed in English, it was over for me. I could not stop laughing. I still had a piece of string that I'd torn from my bookbag stuck between my two front teeth, blowing it out and making hissing sounds. She stormed over to my desk, ripped the floating string from my face, and grabbed my forearm and lead me out of the classroom. She escorted me into the stairwell behind the fire doors, where we were alone. She placed her hand on my neck and pinned me against the wall. She spoke with her teeth touching.

She said, "I could kill you out here right now, and no one would ever know."

I didn't say anything. She threatened my life for disrupting her class! When she finished making her point, we returned to the classroom. Everyone wanted to know what happened. She told the class that we had a secret and then she winked her eye at me. I went on and rolled mines back at her.

I only got to attend middle school for two years because the school systems changed and made ninth grade a part of high school. My time there flew by so fast, but the memories created within those walls are with me forever.

I started driving when I was in middle school. One night on a dare, I stole the car keys from the hook they hung from in the kitchen. Mommy was asleep and Daddy was away. Me, LB, and Shante' hopped in Mommy's Crysler Lebaron and I started it up. LB said, "Let's just go to the stop sign." I put my foot on the brake, moved the gear stick down to the D, placed my hands on the stirring wheel, and slowly raised my foot from the brake pedal. The car started to slowly move. Shante' was in the back seat cheering me on, while LB sat next to me with that same look in her eyes from that time, we got caught hooking school. I knew that meant we were on our way. I drove around the whole Strawberry Hill and back. We parked the car in the same exact spot, and I returned the keys without anyone ever knowing. I'm officially driving at thirteen years old.

Middle school graduation happened and Risha and I was still dressed alike. This time we wore white dresses and our shoes had little heels on them. I was much bigger and curvy by then and being called a brickhouse from the popular Rick James song. Risha hardly changed at all from elementary school. She was still just about her same size.

That summer, Risha and I got our first job. We participated in a summer job program offered by the city. We worked for six weeks and earned three paychecks. We worked as camp leaders at a summer camp for younger kids. The summer camp was in the basement of a huge Church building. Mommy didn't give permission at first because of that. But Daddy stepped in, and we worked those jobs.

Daddy was still spending time running the streets or in jail and Mommy could use the extra income. Mommy was finishing her last year of college and working as an intern, so she agreed to the summer jobs. I made plans about what I planned on doing with all three paychecks, that was going to be in the amount of $201.00 for the first two and the last one in the amount of $189.00. I wanted a ten-speed bike and a pair of skates. I wanted some pants that fit and new shoes. Finally, I wanted a full-length leather coat for high school. Risha didn't make any specific plans on what she wanted to do with her checks. She just did whatever I did, so we had matching everything, including bikes. Risha hated hers and never learned how to ride it. When the six-week summer job program ended, we still had a few weeks of summer break remaining before the start of school. I continued to secretly drive the car to point I had to add gas sometimes. We had a blast that summer meeting people, riding around, smoking, drinking, laughing, and living life. Mommy started to get suspicious, so I scaled back a bit. By the end of that summer, I was ready for whatever. So, I thought.

Mommy graduated from college that year and landed her first job working as an elementary school teacher in one of the elementary schools in Strawberry Hill. She would begin at the start of the schoolyear and would get paid a salary.

Daddy on the other hand, had been diagnosed with an illness. Mommy told us that Daddy had lung cancer and that he was going to become sick at some point. The news of Daddy's terminal illness left me devastated. The thought of losing him terrified me. I prayed for him to get better. Daddy became depressed and eventually, in my eyes, he became a different person for real. A lot of things drastically changed.

Chapter 14 Blip, Blip, Blip

Mommy and Daddy wanted to send Risha and I to the same high schools, but we had very different grade point averages. I had to choose from a city-wide school and Risha had no choice but to attend the high school that was in our neighborhood school zone. China dropped out so Risha wouldn't be able to rely on her in school. Cousin Tricie, Cousin Lia, and I all attended a high school on the West side of town. LB and Shante' attended a different high school on the East side of town. We rode the bus to school together every day because Cousin Lia and her mom Aunt Judy lived with us that year. We would all meet up in the morning to board the bus together and meet up again in the afternoon to go home.

That fall, Daddy started getting sickly. He started to rely on medications and treatment under his Dr's care. He slowed down a lot and he was easily agitated. On his good days, he got out of the house and did what he wanted to do. His condition was up and down for a while. After about a year of treatments, Daddy was admitted into the hospital for long period of time. Maybe a few months.

During that time, Roy was away at the Army Reserves Basic Training. Mommy was in the first year of her new career. China, Risha, and I were at home a lot taking care of things. I was writing more and more, and I had begin making rap songs and performing them at local talent shows. Mommy didn't approve of my liking to music. Hip hop was up and coming. I would go into a zone of my own, when I read my poems over a beat. I thought she was scared for me to fail and be heart broken, because she didn't support anything I was good at. I promised myself that one day I would show Mommy and Daddy my song writing skills and they would be proud of me.

Daddy was released from the hospital near the end of my ninth-grade year. He continued to have good days and then bad days; I was heartbroken, and I wanted him to get better. I learned that Daddy's condition wasn't lung cancer at all. Daddy got caught in the AIDS epidemic that struck our community along with crack in the 80's. I was ashamed and embarrassed to admit it, so I stuck to the story and told anyone who asked that he was sick with lung cancer.

I had changed a lot since he last saw me. In the fall of 1985, my 15th birthday was approaching. China had a baby and put school on hold. Roy got his own place after completing the Army Reserves. I was serious about rapping and I had participated in a few locally hosted talents shows at school and in at events around Strawberry Hill. Risha was still being Risha.

I was a sophomore in high school, when I won a spot in a huge citywide talent show. I had to sell tickets that cost $25.00 each to gain sponsorship. I wrote like I had never wrote before. I practiced and prepared for weeks to perform at the show. I would practice on Roy's Dj equipment that was still set up in his old room while he was away in the Army Reserves. I had the speakers turned up to full blast one day, rapping my heart out. China was in the kitchen washing dishes, Risha was watching tv in the living room and Mommy was out running errands. China yelled at me from the kitchen to turn the music down, but I was in my zone, and I wasn't about to stop.

So, I rapped my reply into the rap song,
"China China,"
"Mind Ya Mind Ya,"
"Own damn business,"
"Before I"
"Find ya, find ya."
~and that's how the fight started.

China burst into the room and charged at me. She snatched the microphone out of my hand and smacked it across my face. She got the blip, blip, blip and hit the floor kicking her feet at me full blast like she was stomping the air. I grabbed one of her feet and when she tried to yank it away from my hands, the strap on her brand-new leather sandals that she paid for with her own summer job check, popped. As the shoe dangled from her ankle, she jumped to her feet and grabbed the box cutter that was lying the on the dresser. She swiftly swiped it across my face. We both froze. I saw blood leaking onto the floor. I pushed pass her and went to my room to take care of my face.

When Mommy got home and found out what happened, I got all the blame. My punishment was that I couldn't perform in the upcoming talent show, and I had to replace China's shoes.

Mommy said, "You're lucky that China didn't kill you."

I was done! The talent show was just a few days away and I had put in so much work for it. I had no choice but to run away from home again. This time I had to really think my plan through because I couldn't get caught.

Chapter 15 Shhh

On the night of my escape, I packed up the essentials, no poems this time and headed over to LB's for a briefing. Another boy from the neighborhood was there at the time and we all sat around for while discussing my plan. The neighborhood boy hung around and worked as the paper boy in the Strawberry Hill. He almost Roy's age, they were friends, so I considered him my friend too. He added his two cents to the conversation. Little did I know, he was spending wooden nickels.

He said, "I know where you could go to lay low for a few days."

We were all ears. He told us about his older brother's studio apartment that he had access to because his brother was in jail and was keeping an eye on the place. He had the keys and he told me that I was welcomed to hide out there and handed me one of the door keys.

It didn't take much more persuasion for me to hop on the bus, ride across town with my bags to that apartment. I had never been inside of a studio apartment before, I stood there thinking, yuk, I would never! It was one small room with a small bathroom in the corner. There was a small bed next to a space heater and a coffee table in the middle of the floor with items placed on top of it and a few bags tucked under it. On the opposite side of the wall, was another small wooden cabinet that held a small black and white tv. The bathroom had a toilet, sink, and a stand-up shower. I turned on the tv and sat down. I pulled out a cigarette and lit up.

A few minutes passed and the neighborhood paper boy was coming through the door using the spare key that he held on to. We were friends so it was cool to have a little company while being a fugitive.

The apartment was in the basement of a big building that housed a Chinese joint on the first level. We got some food and watched some tv for a little while and then he reached for one of the duffle bags that was tucked under the coffee table. The zipper had a small lock on it, but he pried it open just enough to fit his hand inside. He reached his hand inside of the bag and said hold your hands out. I did. He pulled his hand out from the bag clutching a handful of weed. He placed it in my hands. I sat it down and he did it a few more times. He had a small mountain of weed out on the table. I had been experimenting with weed for a little while, so I knew how to roll up and I knew how to smoke. We rolled a whole lot of jays and smoked until I passed out.

When I woke up the sun was shining throw the window and noise from outside was blaring into the room, I got myself together and left with him thinking that we were going to get some food because I was hungry. We never had any discussion, he led, and I followed. I walked with him to the bus stop and when the bus came, we both got on. When the bus reached the downtown area, he stood up and I stood up too. We got off the bus together downtown. We started walking along the street, I wasn't sure to where, I kept going though. After a few blocks, I noticed that he slowed down his stride and was suddenly walking behind me instead of next to me. I looked back one last time and he was dipping into one of the fast-food restaurants as I passed by. He dipped off into the fast-food restaurant and left me stranded. I returned to my house later that day feeling disgusted. I could never tell anyone what happened because I know Daddy would kill both of us for sure! Everyone was worried about me because this had been the longest stay in the history of my running away from home. Mommy never supported the idea of letting me perform in that talent show, but somehow, I did and it was the last.

A few months had passed, and I was in my first semester of 10th grade. Daddy started using a new trial medication for his illness and he was doing better for a while. Not long after my 15th birthday, I was heading out for school. I was running down the steps and Mommy was in the kitchen cooking breakfast. When I got to the bottom of the steps, I suddenly felt an overwhelming need to vomit. I couldn't make it back up the steps to the bathroom, so I headed out the back door. I made it to the edge of our back yard and let it out. Mommy saw the whole thing from the kitchen window. When I came back inside, she had the most humiliated look on her face. I knew what she knew, but neither of us said anything. I went to school. At school that day, I fell asleep in my science class. When I woke up, I was extremely nauseous again. I jumped up from my desk and ran into the restroom at school to vomit. At the end of class, my science teacher approached me and said, "you are pregnant child".

Mommy had Daddy take me to the Dr's. We got in his truck one morning heading to the appointment, Daddy opened a fresh pack of KOOLS as we were leaving the house. When we got to the car, he was already on his 2nd one. The clinic was at the top of Strawberry Hill and by the time we got there, Daddy had finished half of his pack. We left the Dr's office with news that I was 16 weeks pregnant. Daddy was devastated. I was too. I felt like I let Daddy down. I took a wooden nickel. I could never bring myself to tell them who the baby's father was, and they didn't seem to want to know.

Mommy took me to the elders at the club for counsel. She made an appointment at the club for a Saturday afternoon. Seems like the moment the pregnancy was confirmed, my belly popped out for all to see. I can sense Mommy's embarrassment. The private meeting was held in the basement of the club where the elders would meet before Sunday services. They read scripture and stated my consequences. They put me on "public reproof" or something that sounded like that, but it meant that no members of the club could associate with me. The elders didn't ask me about any details of the events leading up to the pregnancy. The fact that I was pregnant at 15 was enough, and I was officially labeled, "bad association". I was on my own from there, I didn't joyfully attend meetings anymore. I had become an outcast, but I prayed anyway. I didn't believe that God agreed with them because I knew that God knew the truth. I prayed for God to stay with me and to forgive me for my acts.

I changed schools so that I could attend the school for pregnant teenagers. Pregnant at 15 was a struggle for me because I got judged, teased, and disrespected on so many occasions. Attending the school for pregnant teenagers helped me cope with the stigma that came along with it. Some of my other pregnant classmates were in relationship with the fathers of their baby's, some didn't know who the father was, and some had already lost the baby's father to violence in the streets. Mommy said the father didn't matter just worry about the baby.

I learned how to prepare for my baby in school. My body went through major transformations when I was pregnant. My vision changed and started wearing eyeglasses that year. I gained 60 pounds. I attended school during the day and worked as a tutor in the evenings so that I could stock up on supplies for my baby. Mommy and Daddy seemed to accept that I was about to be a mother and the beatings stopped, but I still got held accountable in other ways.

I assumed that I was going to have a tough little boy, because I was still a tomboy, and I didn't know what I would do with a dainty little girl. At the baby shower held in school, everyone gave me baby clothes for a boy, and blue items. I had his name picked out and everything. I was going to name him after me but change the first letter for him. God has always proved to me that he is in charge.

On a hot summer afternoon in August, I went into labor. Daddy was nervous and anxious. Mommy laughed at his behavior. After 12 hours of contractions, the push finally came, and I delivered the most beautiful baby girl anyone could ever imagine. She was so beautiful; I had a hard time believing that she was mines, especially since I couldn't compare her to me when I was a baby. When the Dr announced that the baby was a girl, I said, A girl? I was in shock, but I couldn't be happier. Daddy was proud. He told me to take good care of her and finish school! He said that my story doesn't have to go like everybody else's. You got this! Then he looked at the baby and said, "yeah, you gon be good".

She looked like she came from a white woman. Her complexion was very light, and her hair was cold black and full, not a bald spot anywhere on her head. Her hairline formed the shape of a heart in the middle. The rest of her hair was big soft curls that did whatever the hairbrush said. She had perfectly round fluffy cheeks with sharp dimples in the corners. Her eyes were big and bright almond shaped with long lashes and full eyebrows. She had my sideburns slicked down on her tiny little face. Her lips were mines too, sharp, and perky like they were outlined with a pencil. Her ears were big like mines too. She had a hearty appetite, and she would turn pink when she cried. The identity of her father was still my secret, but I promised to tell her about him someday, but not this day. I noticed his nose on her right of way, and when she cried, she looked identical to him. I still didn't say a word to anyone.

On the day I was being discharged from the hospital, the nurse entered my room with a clipboard and some documents. One of the documents was the application for my baby's birth certificate. Mommy was there at time to take us home, and she was sitting there while the nurse completed the forms for me. The nurse got to the part where she needed to know the name of the baby. Until that moment, I still hadn't come up with any names for a girl baby and it had been three days. I looked at my beautiful baby and she was fussing because it was time for a bottle. Her little face was all pink. I looked at the nurse and said that's it. Her name is Pink.

Mommy looked at me with a firm eyeroll and grunted, "Um, Cherry, you can come up with something better than that."

I said yup so her middle name is Ladavious. Mommy was so agitated with me. "Pink Ladavious Heal" is her name, I already knew her last name would have to be Heal because I wasn't married to nobody. The nurse got to the part where the name of the father was. Mommy stared at me with anticipation, I was silent for a few seconds, mind racing. I couldn't do it. I couldn't tell. I saw my life and Paper boy's life flash before my eyes. I snapped out of it and blurted out the first thing that came to mind. I made up a name and the nurse wrote it down. I exhaled, and so did Mommy.

Pink was almost two months old, and I returned to my original high school because my time at the school for pregnant teenagers was up. I was huge, still holding some of the weight I gained while pregnant, but excited to get back into the swing of things with Cousin Tricie and my other friends real at school. It was awkward going back to my original high school to finish up the remainder of the school year. I was different and I simply didn't fit in there anymore. I had mentally matured pass my peers. Cousin Tricie was able to stay and finished up at the city-wide school, of course. I accumulated so many deficiencies, I was sent to my zone school to complete my senior year. LB and Shante' met me there! We all had our senior year of high school together.

Chapter 16 The Truth Can't Lie

Pink was getting big so fast. One day I had her with me across the grass at LB's house.

LB was playing with her like normal and suddenly said, "Aye Yo...",

I said, "yeah."

She goes, "Pink looks like somebody familiar."

I said, "what are you talking about?"

LB stared at Pink a few more seconds and blurted out, "PAPERBOY!"

My cover was blown. LB rolled over laughing at how much Pink looked like him. She wanted to tell him just for his reaction, but he already knew.

I was getting off the bus one day earlier in the week coming home from school, and Paperboy was standing on the opposite corner across the street. It was the first time that I saw him since the incident.

He yelled across the street, "Hey, where's my baby at?"

I kept walking. Later that evening, him and his mom were at our door. Daddy wasn't home at the time. Mommy and his mom talked. I don't know what they talked about, but he was able to have visits with Pink. One day he was late bringing Pink home. When he got to the house, Daddy was waiting on him. I took Pink to my room and turned on my music to drown out the commotion. After that, he didn't come around anymore for long while.

Not long after my 16th birthday, I was allowed to attend a party for one of LB's older sisters because she finished college. The party was a car ride away from Strawberry Hill so I got into the car with LB and her other sister who drove. On the way home from the party later that evening, we got into a terrible car crash and LB's sister's car was totaled.

We all hired the same lawyer who arranged for all of us to get physical therapy sessions for several weeks to treat our non-life-threatening injuries. When it was time for the cases to settle, I had to come to his office with my parents because money was involved. When my lawyer met my parents, he made them sign an agreement to allow me to purchase whatever I wanted with the money if he gave me the check, or he would have to place the money into a trust fund for me until I reached the age of 18. Mommy and Daddy agreed because I had Pink, and they weren't turning down no money. The lawyer asked me what I wanted.

I said, "a car."

I didn't have a driver's license yet, but I had been driving for a few years now. Daddy's eyes got big, and he hesitated at first. But then he said "okay, a car it is". The case paid me $6000. I split it down the middle with Daddy, so my car budget was tight. I started looking for a used car that I could afford to pay for in full.

Roy was back in forth in the reserves and he had a friend who had a car for sale. It had a stick shift gear, but it was in my price range and if it belonged to me, I could certainly learn how to drive it. I purchased my first car! A blue four door ford escort with a hatch back. It reminded of the pinto we had when I was smaller. It was $1800.00. I bought it! I had a car of my own!

Roy promised to give me driving lessons when he got weekend passes, but every time he came home, he would be busy driving my car around without me. He went away for his two-week mandatory stay at the reserves, and I had to take full advantage of my keys. I loved my car. It was the perfect size for me and Pink. She was sitting up now and getting prettier and prettier every day. She was my best friend and I owed her everything!

I got in my car one day, put the key into the ignition, placed my foot on the brake, and turned the key expecting it to start up, like I would do in Mommy's Lebaron. My car abruptly jerked forward, and it didn't start. I thought I broke it. I turned the key again, same thing! I was just about to secretly cry when I looked up and saw a guy from the neighborhood. He came over seeing my dismay and he offered some assistance.

He said, "Oh, this is a stick so you gotta use both of your feet."

He explained how the car worked. I put one foot on the brake, and the other foot on the clutch. I toggled the gear shifter into neutral and turned the key. My car was running! I let it run while he continued explaining to me how my car worked. I pressed the clutch in and moved the gear shifter into the first gear. I slowly raised my foot up from the clutch, while releasing the brake at the same time. My car started to drift forward slowly. I moved my foot from the brake completely and gave it a little gas. The car abruptly jerked forward and scared me, so I slammed my foot back onto the brake. The car cut off. I was shaking like, whew, that was intense! I sat there thinking, how am I going to get my car back to the parking spot now that I broke it for sure?

Ole boy said, "try it again."

I looked at him like did you not just see that? I wasn't sure if the car was even gonna start again but, it did, and I tried it again. I managed to switch gears and I made to the stop sign at the top of the hill. I was at the stop sign a bit longer than I needed to be. I looked in the rear-view mirror and I saw the guy running up behind the car. He knew that I was stuck. Every time I tried to go forward; the car would drift backwards. I would press the brake every time. The car had backed halfway down the hill when he caught up with me. Some other fellas who were standing around, ran over eager to help. They all surrounded the car coaching me on how to drive it correctly. I got it! The rest was history. When Roy returned home from the reserves training, I picked him up from the bus stop in My car. It was bittersweet for him because he had plans, but I was driver now.

My car was a big help! I was able to get to school and work after school. China watched Pink for me because she was finish with school since she had her baby. Daddy got sick again and this time his condition worsened. He started to look sick, and people started spreading rumors that he had "that bug". From the inside looking out, I knew it too. I stuck with the lung cancer story because Mommy never admitted the truth about his diagnosis. Daddy became almost bedridden. I was angry and disappointed in him. I needed him to make different choices and get better for me and Pink. I wanted to show him that he could be proud of me. Most of all, I wanted to see him win, but instead, the drugs got the best of him, and time wasn't waiting.

Chapter 17 High School

When Pink was two years old, I went to a party at the famous music hall in Strawberry Hill. It was the mid 80's and Strawberry Hill was popping. The party was the talk of the town. I borrowed one of Mommy's good dresses that fit. It was fuchsia with black designs all over it, and a bow that tied at the neck. It fit my curves and it was comfortable. I put on a pair of white knee highs and some black shiny shoes. Could not tell me a thang! I pulled up in my car with my friends and parked. We sat in the car for a few minutes checking out the scenery. Then I spotted who I thought was the man of my dreams. He was standing across the parking lot with a group of other boys. They were all from the neighboring community. We locked eyes for a second and I quickly looked away.

LB noticed him too and said, "that's your type yo."

I said, "I know."

LB and I knew everything about one another. We could finish one another's sentences or have a whole conversation without using any words. When we got inside, we found a table and made it ours. We moved back and forth from the food line, bathroom, picture booth, and the dance floor, always returning to our table for check ins.

I sat at the table alone for a few seconds after leaving LB on the dance floor.

I was fumbling around in my purse looking for a joint when a I heard a voice say, "excuse me miss".

I looked up and it was him. Parking lot boy. He was even finer close up. If tall, dark, and handsome was a person, he was standing right in front of me.

I said, "what's up?"

Pretending to be uninterested. I never found myself liking a boy the way I liked him. He was different from the boys in Strawberry Hill. We talked for the rest of the night. We exchanged telephone numbers and began to talk regularly. We had a lot in common. He was a teen parent too. He told me that he had a son with his high school sweetheart, and the relationship didn't work out. We would talk and laugh for hours. We became close friends. I drove to his house regularly sometimes his son would there, and he would play with Pink for hours.

Parking lot boy became friends with Roy too. They had a common hobby, and that was fixing on cars. Roy looked at him like he was the little brother that he wished I was. However, our relationship was stressful, because getting high progressed from recreational/occasional use to routine/regular use. The drug of choice was heroin. It hit the community hard and crack was still around too. I experimented with the hard stuff a few times, but I could never find any sort of fulfillment from it. I never got hooked. I didn't want to go through what Daddy did, so I stayed clear. I struggled to the end of my senior year, and I made it to prom. Parking lot boy and I were on and off because his baby mama still loved him very much. On prom night, Roy was LB's date, and parking lot boy was mines.

WOODEN NICKELS, The Inside Looking Out

    I thought he was going to be the man that I married someday. Until that Sunday afternoon when I went to visit him on short notice. It was the beginning of the last quarter of my senior year, I didn't have my car at the time because it was being repaired and he only lived a few bus stops away. There was a bus stop right in front of his door, so there was no problem getting there. Once I arrived there, Parking lot boy came outside the greet me on his front porch. We hung out there for a little while and then we went inside. When we went inside, his grandmother was in the kitchen cooking food, his mother was sitting at the kitchen table watching tv, and his two sisters were busying around the house fussing, being extra giggly, and asking me silly questions. They were all very nice to me. After a short while, his mom said to him that it was getting late, and I should be getting ready to be on my way.

He said, "ok", and we headed outside.

As we stood on his porch waiting for the next bus, his son came from inside of his house and onto the porch. He was the cutest little boy, and he had his dad's smooth chocolate skin and big curly locks. He was only about four years old.

Parking lot boy looked at him and asked, "What are you doing out here?"

His son replied, "My mommy said come on the inside."

I was so confused, he never mentioned that they were there. The boy and his mom were there inside of the house in the basement the whole time. I was blown away. Parking lot boy followed his son inside of the house and never came back out!

The buses had stopped running and I was stranded. A few hours went by, and he never checked on me. All I could think about was Daddy catching me out there looking like I was stuck holding a pocket full of wooden nickels.

I stood out there until a familiar car came along and stopped at the red light. I heard someone yell my name. It was LB's older sister driving her new car. I was so happy to see her, I ran up to her car, hopped in and went home.

Parking lot boy insisted on making things right with me. He explained that his son's mother had been displaced from her home earlier that day and she didn't have anywhere else to go with his son. She had to live there with him and his family until she got things worked out.

I didn't visit him anymore, but he continued to keep in touch with me. We were friends, I guess. During the final weeks of my senior year of high school, I got into a terrible situation with my English teacher. I had missed his class almost every day that year. It was first period, and I was late getting there most mornings. In the mornings, I had to get Pink up, dressed, and packed up for her long day at China's apartment where she stayed while I attended school.

I arrived late this one morning and he must have been having a rough start. He kicked me out of the classroom as I entered, never allowing me to take a seat. I argued with him as I attempted to leave, and he followed me out into the hallway. He was yelling and screaming at me. He told me to drop out. I told him to quit!

He yelled, "I don't care what assignments you complete; you get nothing but a 50 from me!"

The principal heard the commotion and intervened. He put me out of all Baltimore city public schools, I needed one high school credit to graduate.

I showed up at graduation with Pink on my hip to celebrate for my classmates who made it across the stage. LB and Shante' were among them. I was so proud of them both. After the ceremony, everyone was excited and talking about the different parties being hosted over the weekend. One girl started telling me about her party and noticed that I wasn't wearing a cap and gown. I can't unsee the look on her face to this day sometimes. She looked like she was embarrassed for me. She was definitely hurt. I gave her a hug and assured her that Pink and I were always going to be just fine. I knew that me not walking across the stage with my class had nothing to do with my academic abilities. I promised myself that I would complete college and show that teacher how No weapon formed against me shall prosper, not even his hateful retaliative tactics. I knew that in God's time, I would finish too!

Towards the end of that summer, I noticed that same feeling I had when I was pregnant with Pink. I thought to myself, this can't be. I ignored the feeling and waited some time to see if I was going to miss a period. Time passed, and I did; so, I waited some more time to be sure. I missed my period twice, and I knew why. I kept the news to myself for a while trying to figure out what to do. I told Parking lot boy, and he flipped out. He did not want to have another child at that time. Right before the news, his baby mama had moved out, and he stopped talking to me for a while. He still didn't communicate with me regularly, and I was ok about it. He had already proven that he could never be the type of father to my unborn child that this world required.

Chapter 18 It Keeps Happening

As fate would have it, one day Mommy announces, that we had to move into a regular house because she had steady income, and we could no longer live in the Rows in Strawberry Hill. We moved out of Strawberry Hill, but not too far. Our new house was exactly one block over from where Parking lot boy lived. We moved into a big row home with three bedrooms, a separate dining area, a big basement, fenced backyard, and a deck off the back that attached to the kitchen. I liked the new neighborhood a lot. The stores were a lot closer to the house.

Pink was walking and talking and being a mini me. She was such a cutie, almost old enough to start pre-school which was walking distance away from the house. She was so smart, and I kept her looking like a doll baby in pretty outfits and cute hairdos. Everyone would be in aww at her cuteness.

Daddy was bedridden and his condition was progressing quickly. He needed assistance to get around in the house. He needed assistance using the bathroom, feeding, and bathing. Nurses started to make home visits because Mommy couldn't get him to his appointments anymore. I had paused on school, pregnant with baby number two, and he didn't know. I worked at the local convenient store overnight and took care of Pink during the day. Mommy would usually be gone to work or leaving for work when I got home in the mornings. I would head straight to my room and rest up before Pink woke up ready for breakfast.

This one morning, Mommy was still home when I arrived in from work. I knew something was wrong.

She said, "he's not looking good today."

She was waiting for the nurse to get there. I laid across my bed and dosed off for few minutes when Mommy came in my room waking me up with the news. Daddy was gone. The nurse hadn't got there yet. Mommy notified everyone and people started coming to the house to offer words of sympathy and encouragement. Daddy's body stayed in the house the entire day before the people came to get him out. I was in the dining room when the men carried Daddy's body inside of a burgundy-colored vinyl bag down the stairs and out the front door. Daddy's body bag looked empty, he was so small, but one of the men carried the top and the other carried the bottom. They didn't seem to struggle. Although Daddy's death wasn't unexpected, I wasn't ready for him to go. I was relieved that he didn't have to suffer with his illness anymore, but one month later, his first grandson was born.

     My son came into the world weighing a whopping eight pounds and two ounces. He was so thick and heavy. He had the same fluffy cheeks as Pink, and the same head full of cold black hair. His eyes were puffy, they seemed too heavy for him to stretch them opened. He was so sweet and curious. I couldn't name him after his father because he already had an older brother with that name. So, I found an original name in a book that had a meaning for it, and I gave him that name. However, by the time he started walking, everyone called him Caveman. He was all boy!

By the time he began to walk, Parking lot boy and his family moved to a house at the bottom of my block. He started seeing me with the kids and wanted to come around. I was happy to have him bond with his son. They looked a lot alike, and my son acted so much like him, you'd think he raised him from day one. He would help me out with running errands and stuff, in my car. Parking lot boy turned out be a player.

When his family moved into the house on my block, I saw how he really spent his time. My baby daddy had so many women comings by to visit him, he couldn't keep track of them all. He only remembered one son, when there was five of 'em with three different mamas! He didn't want to come around to bond with his son, he wanted to drive my car around the city and pick up girls.

From the inside looking out, I knew I needed a plan. I had two kids, no diploma, and Daddy was gone. I missed him so much and whenever it got really bad, I would turn on Earth Wind & Fire. I could hear Daddy speaking to me through some of the songs. I'll Write A Song was our favorite. Daddy could hit every note. I worked two jobs, but I earned very little pay because I was young, uneducated, and inexperienced. Some places I worked included the photomat booth, sold perfume, tutored kids, and I even did a few GNA gigs here and there. I hardly had any time to spend with my kids because I had to work all the time. Summer rolled around and my kids were getting big. Pink was enrolled in a pre-school program, and my son was walking and in daycare. I still had my car. Parking lot boy continued to hang out with Caveman in his spare time, but I was off limits! I refused to allow my first-born son to grow up feeling the way I felt when I was his age, rejected.

I was out and about one afternoon when this random guy noticed me. He was dressed in designer labels, jewelry, and expensive sneakers on his feet.

He approached my car and said, "I want you to come see a movie with me later."

Before I could respond to his invite, he reached into his pocket and pulled out a big stack of cash. He started counting out money for me.

He handed me five twenty's and said, "don't say you don't have anything to wear."

Then he did it again. Counted out ten more and said, "don't say you can't find a babysitter."

I was just sitting there confused.

I thought, "Who is this man?"

He continued to shower me with money, and he hadn't even asked my name yet. I thought he was the nicest person that a nice person could be. To top it all off, he then told me that his good friend was a hair stylist and that I had an appointment for that afternoon. I had never experienced anything like that from anybody other than Daddy. I hurried home to get myself together. After I had my hair done, and was dressed in my new outfit, he picked me up from the house and we were off to see a movie.

We became really good friends, and he helped me out a lot financially for a few years. In that time, we became like best friends. He didn't drink or smoke. He just made money. We dressed up and hung out a lot. He spoiled me with what I thought were the finest gifts regularly. Roy was back at home and had taken up residences in the basement. He was different ever since returning home from the army. I continued to work my two jobs, take care of my two kids, and date my balling boyfriend.

In June when school ended for summer break, Mommy made an arrangement for Roy and I to each pay one month's rent, because teachers didn't work in the summertime. Roy was supposed to pay rent for July, and I was supposed to pay rent for August. When July came, Roy didn't have the rent money. Mommy made us switch months, so I paid the rent for July instead. Then, August came, and Roy didn't have the rent that month either. Mommy made me pay it again because I could handle the responsibility. Roy had begun to show more and more signs of addiction the same way Daddy started out. He was unpredictable.

A few days after paying the rent for the second month, LB and I were sitting in the living room watching tv. Roy came in with one of his friends who was from Strawberry Hill too. He came in the door yelling at LB over something somebody said about her on the bus. He tried to put her out of the house. I jumped to her defense. We got into a big fight and tore the whole house up. The next-door neighbor had to call the police. Mommy was furious.

She said, "that's it! You're always just going to be a problem!" and she put me and my kids out.

I celebrated my nineteenth birthday in the comforts of my own apartment. I moved into my first apartment with the help of my boyfriend. Life was happening fast. Too fast when I look back on things. I realize now that God had me the whole time.

When I moved into my own apartment, I made my own rules. I kept it simple, enjoy! I cooked food, played music, and entertained friends whenever I felt like it. I made sure my kids were taken care of and Mommy insisted on regular visits. She received regular gifts too, so she never complained. The following year, I moved to better apartment back in Strawberry Hill. I got one of the private owned apartments for the people who had jobs. I admired them my whole life. I had carpet on the floors and two bedrooms. Every room was furnished nicely. My boyfriend kept the money rolling in, and all was well. Then the bitty's in the neighborhood started hating on how good I was being treated and started laying traps for him.

He got caught. Rumors started circulating that he had another girlfriend in Strawberry Hill, and she also lived in the private apartments for the people who worked. Turns out that he had been two timing me with her for a while and she was pregnant with his twins. The rumors were true. The twins arrived looking like they were really triplets, No denying them! I let her have him. I had my own kids to raise.

Chapter 19 Firm Faith

The jobs with a decent pay required a high school diploma. I had to get mines! I started looking into programs that offered free testing for a high school diploma. All the testing sites wanted me to completed classes before taking the test. I just needed the test, but it was expensive, and I didn't have the extra financial help anymore. I had to apply for government assistance. I was able to get my name on the waiting list for public housing, receive food stamps, and temporary cash assistance. All I had to do was put my kids' fathers on child support. When the lady at the social services office said that part, I changed my mind. I did not want to ask them Ninjas for nothing! Instead, I decided to move back home and reset.

A friend of mines stopped by to check on me one day, because he heard that I moved back home, and I had slowed down a lot. He brought his cousin with him because his cousin David who also grew up in Strawberry Hill, wanted to meet me. I had seen him around but never alone. He would be with a lady every time. He said the same thing about seeing me hanging out with my ex. We started hanging out. Things moved quickly for the two of us, and we saw one another more and more over the next several weeks. The kids liked him too, he didn't have any kids of his own.

Meanwhile, I found out how to get my name up to the top of the public housing list. I went into a homeless shelter for women and spent a few nights, spoke with the outreach people there, and signed up for some programs. A few weeks later, I received a letter from the housing office. I had an appointment. The appointment was scheduled for a date that was just two weeks away. The letter said that at the time of the appointment, I should be prepared to pay the security deposit. That meant, I would leave there with keys. My new friend had a real job. He didn't hustle like Daddy and my ex. He had a schedule. His money wasn't in his pocket, it was on his debit card. He gave me the money for the security deposit so that I could move into my place, without me asking. He offered the stability that my kids and I needed. I was more than excited; I was thankful, and I praised God!

    I never told David that I hadn't completed high school. He just assumed that I did but we never talked about it. From the inside looking out, I saw a bright future for us. We were on the same page. We were going to be that solid couple from straight out of the mud in Strawberry Hill, who our peers could see as a role model. We would grow old together. I wanted to do better because I had be better, and I promised Pink, Daddy, and myself that I would great. David decided to move in with me and the kids after a few months of us dating exclusively. The rent was practically nothing. He worked and I started school at the community college.

He thought I was in college, but I was taking remedial courses to prepare for the high school equivalency exam. I had gotten a little rusty. I became pregnant with baby number three on the way. I snuck and took the high school equivalency test in two separate sessions, on two separate Saturdays. I waited six to eight weeks for the results from the test to come in the mail. I waited on pins and needles hoping that it wouldn't come during a time when David was at home.

The project we lived in was an apartment with two levels. It had one entrance. The front door led to a staircase. At the top of the staircase, was a door. On the other side of the door, was the downstairs part of the apartment. It was an opened floorplan, so it had a kitchen on one side of the room and nothing on the other side but windows. The other door along the same wall as the entrance, but on the opposite end of the wall, led to three bedrooms and bath. I had three bedrooms because my kids were opposite sex. The front door had a mail slot cut out of it. The mail would drop on the floor when it was delivered.

The day that my test results were due, I checked the hallway repeatedly hoping to find a big brown envelop. I was home alone that day. I knew that if a white envelop dropped, it would be a letter reading that I didn't pass. I saw the mailman pull into the court. I ran to the top of the steps, cracked the door enough to see down the stairs to the floor. I saw the mail drop and all white envelops were on the floor. I just stood there for a few seconds disappointed but already praying and thinking about my next move. Suddenly, the mail slot clicked again. I looked down the steps, and I saw my big brown envelop, Thank you God in Jesus name! I did it, I was a high school graduate! I wobbled down the steps and grabbed the diploma. I screamed and cried tears of joy. I yelled, "See Daddy, I did it!" waving the certificate in the air. The next thing I did was register for real college courses.

That next semester, I had my 3rd child and began my college journey. My last son was a gift. We nicknamed him the golden child. Mainly because David was so excited about becoming a dad. His father wanted him from the start. He was named after David, and he was the perfect blend of both of us. He was very light complexed, with a head full of cold black hair with those big soft curls like Pink and his older brother when they were born. He also had the big fluffy cheeks and the small perky lips. He was the most handsome little boy I could ask for.

We were already practically family, and David asked to get married. We announced our engagement and over the next year, planned to have a big wedding in Strawberry Hill at the Multi-purpose building. I continued working to help cover expenses, and I continued to take classes at the community college. I passed all the prerequisites and accumulated enough college credits to advance on as a sophomore. We both had decent paying jobs and we decided to move into a regular house. We gave up the project housing after almost three years. We moved into a house on the same street that Mommy lived on. David's mom was across the way in Strawberry Hill. Everyone got to see the kids whenever they wanted to because we were in the neighborhood again. The expenses changed when we moved into a real house.

David started complaining about bills, so I started looking for higher paying jobs. I was considered in demand due to the facts that I had a clean criminal background, a high school diploma, a clear driver's license, and I was twenty-one years old. I met all the minimum qualifications to be a correctional officer for the State of Maryland. I would receive benefits and perks along with a salary. I applied for the job, and a few months later, I was hired as an officer. I had to complete the police training academy, so I didn't register for classes at the community college the next semester. I graduated from the police academy at the top of my class. My sergeants often bragged on me, for being like a natural on the gun range.

I worked the overnight shift at the only maximum-security prison in Maryland for men. Ironically it was located right next to the yard I grew up running around in. I remember the first time I toured the facility. I thought about when I dreamed of doing this; still processing the fact that I worked at camp! That thought made me chuckle, then in an instant something else dawned on me. For the first time, I thought about Mommy from a wife and mother's perspective.

After working a long shift one afternoon walking along the compound, I became overwhelmed with thoughts of how Mommy made sacrifices to get me there regularly, and how she must have felt being married to a convict. She couldn't have been proud. Back then, I never knew any different. I loved it there because she never complained. Then I wondered why? I shook my head at the thought of it all.

Chapter 20 When God Shows Up

The wedding date was approaching quickly, and I had been a correctional officer for almost a year. I upgraded my vehicle, and a car payment was added to the list of responsibilities. I worked overtime regularly and didn't return to school for a while. Not much later after the wedding, our finances were in order, and David and I purchased our first home together. It was featured on the cover of the weekly nickel saver booklet that I would grab when I went to the market for groceries. It was the curb appeal for me. It was the perfect starter home in my mind, but for David, it his was his dream home.

It was a detached cottage style home on a huge lot with a parking pad. It had blue vinyl siding and a new tree in the front yard. The back yard had a huge tree that provided enough shade to cover the patio no matter where the sun shined, there were beautiful rose bushes that lined front exterior of the house, nestled below the big bay window. The covered front porch was the perfect size to host a small bench, and in the back was a huge, screened porch. On the first floor, was a bathroom, living room, sperate dining room, a small kitchen that led to the screened porch, and two bedrooms. Upstairs was a huge, opened space with storage built in along the walls. The basement had another full-size kitchen, half bath, laundry room with washer and dryer, built in shelving, and ceiling fans throughout. It was amazing!

It was during that time that the term "work hard, play harder" was a word! David remained in his original high school work study assignment and was hired on as a full-time employee after graduation. His schedule was weekdays, 9 to 5. My schedule was four days on, 3 days off, then 5 days on, and 4 days off, with mandatory overtime sprinkled in. I was 23 years old. Married, mother of three school aged kids, working as a correctional officer, and a homeowner. I was literally learning life as it happened. I had my foundation and my faith to guide me through.

I knew early on that David, and I were not on the same path. He didn't believe that prayer worked. We soon understood that we had different plans for our futures. I knew then that I had a purpose to fulfill. I was in the learning life phase and David was finished. He had the wife, house, kids, job, and friends. I was working towards building a better life for us and David was working towards building a better life for him.

At work, my team members and I became a very close-knit group. We could engage in conversations that mattered. We held one another accountable, and we prayed together. We supported one another every day like family. We hung out as a group occasionally because we worked so much otherwise. David spent his time out in bars or with his friends in Strawberry Hill. We became at odds more often as time went on.

I had one teammate who was like the missing pea in my pod. Palmer, but they called her Lil P because she was petite. I was known as C Heal. The moment we met, we clicked for life. Lil P was like the little sister I never had. She was always down for whatever. The jail was our playground. We were there for the money. We routinely worked double shifts back-to-back. I worked my normal overnight shift and then I'd stay for the day shift. I would get home in time to greet the kids from school, David from work, and get a little rest.

David started resenting my new lifestyle of working so much and meeting new friends. He started to complain a lot more and drink heavily. We had a fully stocked bar in the basement, and he would retreat down there daily. His friends would come over and sometimes they would bring their dates with them because it was such a comfortable place. Some of his married friends would show up with women who weren't their wives. David would see me off to work while still entertaining guest. David would keep secrets for them and make their wives think that he was a creditable witness.

As time went on, David started openly seeing other women too. Eventually, he got really disrespectful. He was openly seeing women and embarrassing me in public. He became mean and insulting me was his norm. We would stop talking sometimes for weeks at a time, and I threatened to leave him.

He became so controlling that one night I went out to a party with my work friends. David wanted to know my location. We weren't talking so he tracked my phone.

My team was gathered at the table laughing, drinking, and having a good time, when David walks through the crowd wearing pajamas and slippers, yelling, "where's my wife!?"

Lil P saw him first and said, "Aye Yo, I know that ain't that Ninja."

It was. He spotted us and made his way over to our table.

He looked at me and aggressively asked, "Can I have a word with you?"

Lil P responded, "No the f*ck you cannot!"

He replied, "Bitch, I'm not talking to you".

My other team members all looked up, and quickly headed our way like a signal was called on the tier.

One of them whispered to David, "You don't want this Bro".

He was peacefully escorted out of the building. The drama between us went on for years. He continued to be a habitual cheater. I was extremely unhappy.

The final straw was when he got reacquainted with his high school sweetheart. We were about nine years into the marriage, and we were referring to one another as roommates. I was with him the day he spotted her walking down the street. I sat right next to him in the car. I watched his body language and his facial expression exude excitement. He jumped out of the car and ran up to her to say hello. They talked for a few minutes as I patiently waited, and then he returned to the car.

He looked at his phone still smiling, and said, "yeah that was my baby in school, yes sir, mm, mm, mm, she still looking good."

Then he snapped out of it, and said, "we just old friends, don't be mad because people love and respect me."

Then he went into his long rant about how he was the greatest of all times because he was still holding down his work study job. He wanted her to know that because other people from school are out there messing up. Funny how he went on responding to unasked questions. I never said a word, just listened. The two of them rekindled what was forgotten back in high school. Apparently, he was more attractive in her eyes now he was a grown man with a wife, a big house, two cars, nice clothes, and extra cash to throw around. He claimed that she wouldn't give him the time of day when they were in high school.

They started openly dating, and she got pregnant. He moved into her apartment with her and her two kids. He was picking the kids up and taking them to her house for quality time. I would run into her at markets or other random places while out, and she would look at me like she won. Eventually, he stopped allowing Pink and Caveman to come along on the quality time visits. He explained that he only wanted to deal his own kid. By then, I filed for legal separation with plans to divorce. The kids were already heartbroken. He wanted to move his new love into my house. He fought for the house in court claiming that it was more his than mines for some odd reason. The judge granted me use and possession of the house for three years and then I would be on my own.

He stayed with her during her pregnancy and had a baby shower hosted at his mother's house. His mother was always supportive of his decisions, no matter what they were.

They invited Cousin Tiricie to the baby shower, and yes, she did attend...She reported back to me that my wedding pictures that once hung on her living room wall had all been replaced with pictures of David and his new soon to be baby mama.

He had final divorce papers served to me one random afternoon. Before the divorce was final, she delivered the baby. I found out while driving through Strawberry Hill one afternoon, and he was standing outside of his mother's house talking with some guys. As I attempted to drive by, he waved me down asking me to stop. I pulled over and he tried to show me a piece of paper that he held in his hand. I asked him what it was, assuming he was about to show off baby pictures. I could not believe what this negro told me. He looked in my eyes and dang near whimpered that the baby was not his! I just pulled off...Wooden Nickel ass Ninja! Poof, Be Gone! I prayed for him though.

After the divorce, I continued working as a correctional officer for a few more years. David remarried a new love interest shortly thereafter. Lil P and I established ourselves and the convicts didn't give us any trouble. One morning after finishing up a double shift and preparing to return eight hours later to do it again, a convict slipped me a kite that read, stay home. I knew what that meant, and I put the team on notice. I went home to get some rest. When I woke up in time to get dressed for work again, I turned on the news. I was in shock when I saw a full riot in progress at the prison. The convicts had taken over the prison. Officers got hurt and so did a lot of convicts. The National Guard had to come in to assist with regaining control of the prison. The prison was on lock down for a few years after the riot, and it was harder and harder spend so much time in there every day. It was time for a change. Like always, I didn't see it coming.

  I wanted to do something different that would offer me more personal fulfillment, and of course be a bit safer. My kids were getting older and so was I. I thought about returning to school, but it wasn't possible. I weighed my options. I still didn't have any real work experience and I needed a job that I could enjoy and that paid enough money to cover my expenses. I reminded God of all these things in my prayers, and I asked him to please guide my steps.

  I started on plans to open my own daycare business in the basement of the house. I did some research and took the necessary classes. I set up the basement with all the required safety equipment and supplies, installed a play area in the backyard, and drew up contracts for my customers. It was very nice!

I applied for my daycare license, but I hadn't received any updates on the status of it. Meanwhile I kept pushing forward with plans, and I had a waiting list of kids ready to start. It was holiday season and Lil P got into some serious trouble outside of work. The badge couldn't protect her this time, and she got fired. I heard the news after the fact. When I found out that Lil P was fired, I quit. I couldn't do it without her there. I left the job that night and without calling ahead joined her at our favorite bar, I already knew where to find her. She looked up and saw me standing there, we just burst out laughing. She knew that I quit without me saying. I confirmed, "No P, No C." we continued laughing and celebrating our new freedom.

Chapter 21 One Prayer

I waited until I got home later and thought about the consequences of my actions. I could only talk to God about it. I prayed and went to sleep. I woke up feeling renewed. I did my normal morning routines. I took the kids to school and stopped pass the grocery store on the way home. I didn't have any plans because I no longer had a job. I pulled up to my beautiful home and stared at it. I thanked God as I sat in car. I was taking my time going inside because I saw the mailman coming. I wanted to grab the mail before I went inside so that I wouldn't have to come back outside any time soon. I wanted to nap. I got out of the car when the mailman reached my house. We exchanged greetings, and he handed me my mail. I didn't look at it until I got inside. I almost took my nap first, but I noticed that one of the envelops was a bit larger and fancier than the rest. I flipped to it. It was from the daycare board.

I paused and said, "no way, God, no way!"

I opened it and I had a license to operate my OWN business!

The very next day, I did. I worked on my signed and hung it out on the front porch. My home was now an official place of business, and business was good!

I easily earned a little over $70k in my first year of business. I kept it going for a few years. I was single, and independent with big responsibilities. I dated here and there but nothing serious.

I focused on financial stability and keeping my kids happy as David harassed us constantly. He was angry for years because he had to pay child support for Jr. He would cuss me out and disrespect me in front of the kids and anyone else. My dad would be ashamed of me if he knew that I was accepting that treatment from somebody's dusty ass son. I finally snapped on him one day. I put him in his place and let him know that if he didn't speak to me with the same respect he receives when I speak to him, then we will **NEVER** speak again! He got the message loud and clear, he's been respectful ever since.

Working at home with a normal schedule and a livable income, I was ready to return to school. I wasn't sure about what I wanted to study so I focused on finishing up all the general study courses first. I started taking classes at night. I would drop the kids off to Mommy's house after work and pick them up after class. I usually would finish up around 10:00 at night. Pink was in high school, and she had a boyfriend, Caveman was having behavior concerns at school, and Jr was feeling confused because David unintentionally of course, created a triangulation among the kids. They were a handful. I struggled to find balance.

Then when Pink was 16 years old, she got pregnant with my first grandson I was 31 years old myself. I was overwhelmed. It was time for a change. I wasn't ready, but I was. The last thing I wanted is for Pink to go through what I went through as a teen aged mother. It's not for the weak! I had to go harder than ever before so that Pink could always count on me whenever she needed to. My daycare was doing good, but I started to feel burnout from spending so much time in the house. I routinely did research job descriptions that matched my abilities. Something LB taught me because she worked as a job facilitator for the state, and she knew a lot about getting hired. I came across a job description for a customer account executive. I liked the title, so I continued reading. The description matched and I applied.

I took a pay cut but I was still able to cover my monthly expenses and I received benefits. The job offered an onsite fitness center and a cafeteria that featured healthy menu options. The benefits grabbed my attention.

I was still struggling with weight that I never loss after having children. I wanted to upgrade my quality of life. After receiving health care coverage, I qualified for weight loss surgery. On surgery day, I weighed 307 pounds. My knees buckled and I suffered with back pain. I had a procedure that reduced the size of my stomach to the size and shape of a banana. The procedure went well, and I went from a pants size 24 down to a size 18 in a few months. I made a full recovery and returned to work.

Not long after my recovery, Pink was expecting baby number two. As time went on, finances got tight, and I had no choice but to file for bankruptcy in pursuit of a new start. The house had to go too. I thanked God for the time we spent there, and faithfully prepared to accept whatever was next. I moved into an apartment and continued taking classes at night, while focusing on my weight. For the next couple of years, we moved around between different addresses, because I was in survival mode. There were times I just didn't know if we would be alright, but we always were. I was working two jobs and some semesters I could only squeeze in one or two classes, but progress was being made. Caveman was now 16 years old, and he was in the streets a lot.

One day I was at work and Pink called me. She was had urgent news and I had to step outside to take the call.

She said, "Ma, you gotta come to the hospital right now."

I should have panicked, but I remained calmed.

I asked, "what's going on?"

Pink goes on to say, "You remember the girl I used to hang out with a while back named Kita?"

I said, "No. Why should I remember her?"

Pink says, "she just had Caveman's baby and she already got an opened investigation with CPS involving her first two sons, so the people are here to take the baby from her and place him into foster care if we don't claim him right now!"

I said, "What!?"

She repeated the whole thing for me. I clocked out and headed to the hospital.

When I arrived, the people from the agency were there just like Pink told me. They were waiting for me to get there so they could interview me. I wanted to see the baby.

I went into the hospital room, and I immediately recognized Kita. She was a few years older than Caveman. I was floored, but I stayed focused. She was crying hysterically yelling about how they took her baby from her womb, and it wasn't fair. I could feel the agony she was experiencing. My heart melted for her and her baby.

The baby was in the hospital's basinet next to Kita's bed. I walked over to it and stood there staring at what could have literally been Caveman all over again. He had all the same features that Caveman was born with.

I said, "My God."

I didn't even know Caveman's where abouts at the time. He was running around in the streets with his friends obviously being hot! Before that day, I had no idea she was expecting a baby, let alone Caveman's baby. The people from the agency said they would have to complete a background check and once cleared, we could take the baby home from the hospital. We headed to the store to pick up supplies. The results were back in 24 hours. I brought my grandson home from the hospital at four days old. Kita named him Cason, thinking it was my son's government name. When I saw the name on his birth certificate, I just shook my head.

In the months to come, I went back and forth with the dept of social services because they wanted me to remain involved with them and receive financial support for Cason. I declined, that would be like hustling backwards for me. We're good. In court, they assigned a public defender to Cason's case, and he was supposed to be on our side. However, the attorney's debriefed in our absence and they had already determined that Cason would remain, "a child in need of assistance", and he would get that financial support and other benefits provided by the agency. The benefits included home visits to ensure that all is well and supervised visits from his mother. My son was 16 years old, and we did not have the capacity to abide by those restrictions. So, we agued our own case in front of the judge and we won!

The judge asked Caveman how he spent time with Cason when they are at home. The courtroom was silent with anticipation of Caveman's response.

Caveman said, "when we're at home, I give him baths, make his bottles, change his pampers, wash his hair, keep him spelling fresh, and make sure he doesn't fall off the bed. The people in the courtroom showed compassion for Caveman and Cason. The judge agreed that with the support of me and Pink, Cason would be just fine. Cason was officially the newest member our family. That same year, Jr had started high school. We adjusted along the way. After all, this wasn't my first rodeo.

The years passed by quickly. In no time all Pink was married with four kids, one son and three beautiful daughters, Caveman had 3 sons, they had their own places, and Jr was off perusing his studies in college. I had a total of seven grandkids! I worked full time during the day and attended school full time in the evenings. My weight was a stable 220 pounds, but I carried well. I was renting an affordable row house, and my minivan was paid for. I lived alone and didn't have to worry about anyone but myself.

Chapter 22 For Much is Required

I had returned to college when I met Greg, husband number two. It was during the point in my life where I was willing to compromise. Since I was in the process of developing myself into the best version of me, I figured that it would be okay to deal with a man who was also in the process of developing himself into the best version of him. I gave myself permission to settle. Husband number two was the opposite of David.

He was rough and rude to people who he needed to be that way with. But he was also kind and thoughtful to most. He was charming. When I told him my name, he called me Cherry Pie.

I asked, "You like cherry pie a lot or something?"

He said, "No, it's my last name, Greg Pie spelled P-y-e."

I thought "Wow, funny too?"

He was recovering from drug addiction and had a few years of clean time. He had that fresh out prison fitness on him. He worked on cars and told me that he had his own shop where he operated his business. He reminded me of Daddy. He helped me imagine how Daddy would have been if he had the chance to get clean. I wanted to help him.

For the first few months, we got to know one another better. He seemed like he was going to reach his full potential, and I was willing to stand by his side to assist. We spent a lot of time together doing things he'd missed while he was using. We went on road trips, vacations, sporting events, and other social activities. After only a year and a half of dating exclusively, we got married. Things took a turn on the night of the wedding!

We had a small ceremony in a hall for rent that was located at end of the block we lived on. Jr came home from college for that weekend so that he could attend the wedding. After all the festivities were over, close members from both of our sides of our families, including LB and Cousin Tricie, came to back to our house with us to continue celebrating. We weren't flying out for the honeymoon in Las Vegas until the next morning, and we wanted to open gifts.

We were all gathered in the living room talking and looking at pictures. I was about to get started on opening gifts when Jr said he needed to tell me something. He said he was trying to work on a paper due when returned to school, but his laptop was missing.

I said, "No way, I'll help you look for it."

I started moving things around looking for the missing laptop. People noticed that we were looking for something and joined in. Caveman got frustrated and said, he was about to start checking people. We couldn't find it anywhere. Caveman started looking around at people in the room. Jr was devastated thinking about not finding it. Suddenly, after Caveman's face check, he confronted a suspect. It was my new husband's nephew. Caveman figured out that he stole the Jr's laptop during the wedding reception and had someone come by to get it. The nephew denied and raised his voice. Caveman advanced towards him and told him to get out. He refused, yelling back at Caveman, "I ain't going nowhere!" There were no more words.

One of my cousins grabbed his ass so quick and threw him out the back door. Caveman ran out behind them followed by everyone else. The brawl grew when it reached the backyard. Somebody started cutting, somebody else started throwing things, and the police were called. When it was all over, my dress was ripped, my new husband had a broken leg, and we never found the laptop. We went to Las Vegas the next morning though, broke leg in all.

The rough start of our marriage wasn't enough warning for me to get out of it then. We replaced Jr's laptop, and everyone made amends. Greg registered for classes so that he could earn his high school diploma, but he never completed any because he claimed that he was always working on cars. I finished college and received my bachelor's degree in business administration and management. It hit me like a Mack truck one day when I was out shopping for my graduation outfit.

I was in the fitting room trying on a dress. I looked at myself in the mirror and thought about the occasion. I said to myself, "WAIT...DID I JUST FINISH COLLEGE???? OH MY GOD, MY GOD, THANK YOU!!!" Suddenly, I broke out in full praise! When I came out of that dressing room, my face was still wet from my tears of joy, and people were standing around clapping and congratulating me. One lady slipped me a five-dollar bill and said congratulations. I felt so accomplished and proud of myself, but I was sorry that Daddy didn't get to see it. I wrote this poem to celebrate...

Oh Yes, I Did!

Oh My God... I got through it.
I stopped thinking about why I needed to do it.
I was wondering how many people knew that.
So many times, I wanted to say screw it!
But it would've been too easy to just stop and quit.
It was too late; I was in too deep with it.
I already written so many papers,
Stayed off the grass, no more weed vapors.
At the end of this tunnel there would be a bright light,
So, I just kept staying up night after night.
See I came from a GED.
No traditional education for me.
But I have kids that I have to lead by example.
I had to show them that my GED was just a sample,
Of what can be done when you put your mind to it.
One day at a time and you to will be through it.
I needed to write this message to say,
Just how it feels to be faced with graduation day.
It is a great accomplishment like no other.
To me it's like becoming a wife or a mother
I smile so hard my cheeks start to ache,
My eyes fill up and my knees shake.
College graduation is the happiest time of my life.
It was worth every minute, despite the strife.
At the end of the day in my prayers before bed,
I say to myself, Oh Yes, I Did!

Greg still hadn't begun his classes when I started my next salaried position at the trade schools. It was then when I noticed a shift in his behaviors. My new job also provided me with tuition reimbursement. I took full advantage of the opportunity. I enrolled full time taken graduate courses in business management and administration. At the time, I still simultaneously contemplated on what my purpose was, and how could I find balance between self-fulfillment and financial gain. My load was heavy with my children and spouse. I completed countless research papers and reports after work. For much is required! I would try to engage Greg in studies hoping he would be motivated to begin his GED classes, instead he grew envious. He made himself busy with outside things and I didn't bother to concern myself. I already knew where this was going. I gave it to God in prayer and focused on my studies.

When Cason was in 1st grade, he started struggling with behavior problems like Caveman did when he was in school. I was in a better position to help this time and I stepped in. I started visiting the school to see what was going on.

Cason was in school being a completely out of control most days. He would disrupt the class and fight on kids. He was angry. I moved him in with me and transferred him to a better school. I had him evaluated for possible learning or developmental disorders. He was diagnosed with ADHD and depression. When he turned 7, he started taking medication to keep him calm during school. However, he continued to have meltdowns and cause disruption. He reminded me of me at his age, but I rocked on the chairs. I attended his IEP meeting and that's when I knew what I wanted to do with my career. Cason's IEP team members had the same energy as my high school teacher. They were not interested in Cason's academic success; they were collecting their paychecks. The meeting did not end well. The team insisted that Cason continued to rely on medication in order to attend school every day, after they all agreed that even when he was medicated, the behavior does not change. I understood what Cason was experiencing when he was surrounded by these people.

During the meeting the IEP chair said to me, "we don't do this kind here."

I contemplated taking a charge in that moment, but I simply excused myself from the meeting and had Cason transferred to a school in the Charter systems. On the way home I promised Cason that someday, I would be in that same seat doing that same job! I was convinced at the time that I had discovered my life's purpose. I am going to be an Educator! Not just any educator. I'm going to make a difference!

Chapter 23 He'll Make it Alright

My job offered tuition reimbursement so the next term, I registered for graduate school in pursuit of a master's degree in education. From the inside looking out, I knew my life was about to change in ways that I only could imagine.

I trained as an urban teacher specifically because I wanted to work with kids who had backgrounds like my own. In my first semester, my class had to conduct a case study on the results of education on kids raised in poverty. During the lecture, the professor begins to state some facts about a community in the city that was segregated all the way up to the early 80's. My classmates were not Baltimore natives, so it was history for them. She went on to say that there was a completely Black occupied community with stores, clinics, libraries, schools, and churches. I sat there listening to her, and I could easily visualize Strawberry Hill. So, when she said something about the clay mountain, I blurted it out.

I said, "You're referring to Strawberry Hill".

Everyone turned and looked at me. I suddenly realized that I was among people who had no idea of what poverty was. Most of my classmates were young fresh out of college kids, new to the city and white. They were about to learn about Strawberry Hill from a textbook using artifacts like Black & white photos, from my hood as reference. I felt like I was on a prank video.

My professor asked me, "what do you know about it?"

I said, "I was born and raised there."

Everyone just stared in silence like they were looking at Harriet Tubman or someone like her. From the inside looking out, I was stuck on the fact that Strawberry Hill was a topic for case studies in graduate school. I was thinking I would end up discovering my baby picture messing around with these folks. I was feeling like a primary source of information for my classmates. Then came time to produce a written product. My information was good, but I lacked the abilities to produce a scholarly written product. I struggled to do better but I was missing the mark.

One day, my professor pulled me aside for a critical conversation. She explained to me how my writing would improve if I just gave them exactly what they asked for. Nothing extra. She informed me that my information was too transparent for the young incoming teachers. My papers were full of slang and jargon. They didn't need to know how the free cheese wasn't so bad, or that we cleaned the community ourselves, or that we hosted our own talent shows, and that we survived. The goal of the study was to prepare the new teachers for the confirmed behavior challenges that they would be faced with in City schools. I disagreed because I knew firsthand that Strawberry Hill was a great place to grow up, and the outcome depended on choices made with the resources provided for me.

My classmates were able to use information in their papers citing me as the primary source. I on the other hand tried to do the same thing, but I couldn't be my own source. I was internalizing it as a personal attack. I prayed about it and decided to listen more so that I could hear! I took a learner's stance. I learned that the early education I received in Strawberry Hill provided me with early literacy and math skills setting the tone for my academic future. I discovered that Strawberry Hill was historical and was being talked about in graduate school. The community is still thriving today because it's cared for and occupied with many original residents and business owners from the 70's and earlier.

While the case study proved that individuals had to go against all odds to make it out, many former residents did it. I am a product of that educational system and today, I still sat at the same table, taking the same courses, and learning the same information with classmates who didn't have the same set of circumstances as myself. They were learning about poverty, from a textbook. I was learning about prosperity from the stories they shared about their parents. One day while on our lunch break, me and a few classmates drove over to Strawberry Hill to see if we could find one of the tags I made in the cement when I was a kid. They followed me to my old elementary school's playground. The school had been closed for renovations for some time and it looked abandoned. But the old swing set was still there. In my mind I was thinking, it's been decades since I had been here. I felt old and big. We went up to the door of the school building and the original pavement was still there. I could hardly believe my eyes when I saw, Cherry was here! Inside of a heart, just as I had left it decades earlier. We were all amazed. I wanted that to be the paper!

I was in my second semester of graduate school, when Jr finished college. The kids and I all drove out to the college campus to attend his ceremony. David was there with his new wife, Greg was there with me, Mommy and all the grandkids were there too.

During the ceremony, we watched from the window of Jr's dorm room until it was time for the degrees to be handed out. It was about 100 degrees outside and even hotter under that pavilion where the chairs were. The door to the dorm room was propped open for ventilation but the heat still radiated up the stairs that led to the living area of the dorm. The courtyard was full of people hanging around celebrating the occasion. We heard the announcement that we had been waiting for. It was time for Jr to receive his bachelor's degree in computer science. He was always extremely intelligent and far ahead of his time, living up to his childhood nickname, the golden child.

I headed out first, Pink and Caveman next, then a few other people after them. Greg was already outside and so were the kids. I had one hand on the rail as I walked down the stairs. I got halfway down the steps and attempted to make another step when my foot didn't move as I advanced forward. It was like something under the steps held on to my foot or something. I heard a snap that sounded similar to a crispy fried chicken wing being separated at the gristle.

I was scared to look. I slowly lowered my body down into a seated position on the step that I stopped on. Briefly, I thought I saw my entire foot was turned around backwards like it was being screwed off. I never looked at it again. I immediately gave instructions to everyone in proximity. I was not messing around! I prayed for a full recovery, and it was on and popping. Someone called the paramedics. They were on sight already, but several emergencies were happening at the same time as my injury, and I had to sit there for quite a while. I didn't budge. I had Caveman cover my foot so that I wouldn't mistakenly get another look at it. He tried to hide his face, but I saw that he was crying. Pink told me later that he threw up too. I reassured him that I was okay.

The EMS arrived and didn't know what to do. They were both young and inexperienced. When they lifted the sheet and looked at my foot, they were nervous about carrying me down the remaining steps. I had sat there long enough to already have it figured out. I had Caveman get another sheet because this would require two. I placed one of the sheets under my foot and used the other one to carry it. I was able to stand on my good foot and hop to the stretcher. I missed Jr being handed his degree. My ankle was broken in four places and completely dislocated. Greg wanted to know who to sue. All I wanted was a full recovery and that was my prayer.

I would need to spend all summer recovering. Greg was at an all-time trifling. He was outside getting his life while I was confined to the house gaining weight and feeling depressed. I gained all my weight back quickly. I missed some course work at the start summer, so as the fall semester was drawing near, I was feeling discouraged about finishing. I had been placed on non-weight baring status for three months by my doctor, and my school was advising me to sit the year out. They said there was no way that I could get caught up and finish in that condition. I was supposed to begin my first year of student teaching that fall, and my assignment was at one of the elementary schools in Strawberry Hill. It was the one that Cousin Tricie attended when we were small. I felt that it was literally God's intention for me to begin my teaching career there. I prayed about it and focused on recovery.

One day, a classmate came by to check on me. I had been struggling all morning. I was home alone, and I was trying to fix something to eat. I was low on groceries and all I had a bag of frozen breaded chicken wings in the freezer. I was moving around the apartment in my big awkward wheelchair and managed to get the chicken onto a pan and into the oven. I couldn't break them apart though because I was balancing myself to avoid further injury.

The chicken overcooked and it looked like a pile of something unrecognizable, but I was hungry. When my classmate saw my meal, she called some more classmates, and they all pitched in with support. I needed help and I didn't know how to ask for it. God sent them my way. I turned the radio on and the song by Erica Campell was playing.

We both broke out in song, "IIIII just can't give up now...I've come too far from where I starrted from... Nobody told me, the road would be easy, and I don't believe he brought this far to leave me!

As God would have it, I completed the whole semester on a knee scooter. I drove to class with my right foot and wore a big boot that I had to put on and take off to drive. When I reached the point where I could put partial weight on my ankle, and I begin to walk again while wearing a boot. I wore that boot all that year. I had made a full recovery, just in time to walk across the stage. I walked with no boot, with my cohort of highly intelligent peers on time, for the first time, across the stage to receive not one, but two master's degrees! Ain't NO way I could have done that alone! I know that was God's work. I achieved what I had always prayed for and only dreamed of. I earned a total of three college degrees! I was blessed with one for each of my kids!

I wrote this poem to mark the moment. I titled it Thank You Mr. Ready after the high school teacher that I suddenly wanted to find right away! It went like this:

Thinking back to 88, Mr Ready was out the da gate!
He said, Ion't care what grade you make, you will NEVER graduate!
Why don't you just drop out, Sh*t!
Drop out sh*t, how bout you quit!
These were the exact words between me and my teacher.
1988 and this was the feature.
12th grade, 4th quarter,
Me, bad attitude, and a baby daughter!
Ummmmm
Fast forward, it's now 2016.
Trials and errors...Life has been so mean!
But through it all, I kept my FAITH.
Stayed prayed up and life got straight.
Mr. Ready will never understand how his words influenced me.
All I know is today I have THREE COLLEGE DEGREES.
That's right, 1 BA, and 2 M. Ed's
So, thank you Mr. Ready for motivating me!

Greg had really gone off the deep end by then, and I knew that God would intervein. Our short marriage came to an abrupt halt. He stopped contributing to the expenses all together, his shop wasn't his shop, and he didn't have any documentation of any formal training in auto repair. All these years later and still no traction on becoming the best version of himself. He was a big Wooden Nickel!

On the morning of New Year's Day, I was cleaning up from the party we hosted that night before to bring in the new year. I discovered a gun that someone left behind. It was a long nose forty-four, nasty! Greg told me that it belonged to a friend of his, and he was going to return it to the friend later that same day. I had already placed it safely into a bright colored vinyl school bag that I had laying around. It was easily recognizable and secure.

He left the house with the bag supposedly headed to work. He was gone all day and I hadn't heard anything from him. Later that evening, I was reading over old emails, and I noticed repeated emails from the cell phone provider. I had the account on autopay, so I never opened the messages. I assumed they were all payment confirmations. But I had time on that day, so I opened the most recent one sent. It was an alert that one of the phone lines on the account had exceeded the data and I was being billed additional charges. I was taking care the phones for Mommy, Cason, Greg, and myself. I knew it wasn't Mommy's line because she could barely open her text messages without asking somebody to help her work her phone. I automatically assumed it was Cason's line. I clicked on his line, and it wasn't him. He was well below the limits. I paused, not assuming anything at all, then I clicked on Greg's line. It was his line consuming all the data. I wondered how, what could he possibly be doing that would eat up data like that?

I clicked again. I noticed a telephone number listed over hundreds of times in the conversation tab. It looked like it could have been an error. I wondered if he was consulting with someone about cars or something. Cheating was the last thing that I suspected. He was only a catch in my eyes.

I continued reading, to see what the messages were about. I clicked on one of the messages. It was from a woman. I continued clicking to be sure that I wasn't tripping. I wasn't. As I'm reading the messages, he walks in. I ask him about the messages, and he waved me off, went up the steps and went to bed. I kept reading. I wanted to know exactly what I was dealing with. He had an ongoing relationship with a younger woman and his whole family was in it. I thought, this is nothing but the lesson.

I said, "thank you God, message received."

I called LB and told her what happened, and she came over to help me plot things out. We read all the messages and by the next day we knew her name, age, address, and who she hung out with.

LB said, "He can take the window or the stairs".

We laughed as we planned to pack him up as soon as he left for the day. LB went home real late that night and I was going to let her know when the coast was clear in the morning so that we could get it done. I ended up sleeping late and I woke up with a slight headache. Instead, I told LB we could hold off until a little later. Meanwhile, she trolled social media and had something to say about all the girl's pictures for entertainment.

It had gotten late when I pulled myself together and I decided to make a cup of tea. The alarm code was changed earlier that day and I forgot to change it back since we postponed the plan. It never dawned on me that Greg received an alert from the alarm notifying him that there had been a change to the access code.

When he came home, he came into the kitchen while I was standing at the stove. In my peripheral, I could see that he was carrying my bright colored vinyl school bag that he took with him the day before. I remained calm, but my mind instantly went into survival mode. Cason was upstairs sleeping, and I needed to temperature check this fool. I slowly turned around to look him in his eyes. They were bloodshot red, he was drunk, and maybe high on something. I had seen that look before, just not on him. I watched him for a few seconds. At this point, there's a stranger in my house!

He burst out and yelled, "I ain't going no f*cking where!"

He wanted a reason.

I heard the word, "stand".

I didn't know where it came from, but I listened. I didn't move or say a word. He was confused. He grabbed the bag, turned around, and went upstairs. I slowly walked behind him and watched his movements. He went into our bedroom and slammed the door shut.

I calmly called Cason's name and he appeared at the top of the steps.

I said, "come on."

We left the house. I drove across the street to the shopping center parking lot and called the police. I told the police that I found a gun in my back yard, and I wanted to turn it in. They were suspicious and asked more questions. The police asked me if someone was in the house, and I said, yes, my husband was sleeping. They arrived to retrieve the gun.

Greg had it fully exposed on my pillow. He had fallen asleep with it next to him. Protocol required a trace of the gun's serial number, and when it came back as stolen, they had to run our IDs too. Gregg had a felony, so he was arrested. While being taken into custody by the police, he threatened too unalive me. He was denied bail and by the time he was released, we were legally divorced.

The next time I saw him, he was on social media playing with his newborn baby girl. God had my back the whole time. I didn't need to plan; God knew his time was up. I got stuck with his last name because at the time of graduation it was my legal name, and it was printed on all my credentials. To this day I am Cherry Pye. God has a sense of humor too.

Book 3
Butterfly & Flying

Chapter 24 Problem

I really can't recall which came first, the funeral or the news. I do remember what I was wearing, the house I lived in, and the room we all gathered in when it officially got real. I was wearing my blonde wig because it was late spring heading into summer. I wasn't wearing a jacket. My shoulders were out. My two-piece matching floral print jogger suit paired great with my lace textured sneakers and was the perfect fit for my long day of driving Lyft and Uber. I was on break from my full-time job as a schoolteacher for a few days and I could never keep still so I was outside making money. The weather was fantastic! The sun shined brighter than usual compared the previous days.

I knew that we had just lost Cousin Daisy, and the funeral services was happening on this day. While driving, I ended up around the area where the funeral services being held, and I decided to stop in to pay my respects. The funeral services were being held at a funeral home, so Mommy was in attendance. I knew she was going to give me a sharp side eye the moment she saw me because I wasn't dressed appropriately, and I was late. *Always a problem.* I was stopped, and questioned by security at the door before I was allowed entry. I walked into the sanctuary oddly surprised of the large amount of people there. The room was still and silent. People were viewing the body. I walked up the center aisle to join the end of the slowly moving viewing line, passing family members and strangers along the way. As I got closer to the opened casket, I started to feel this enormous heaviness over me. I felt like I was being weighted down from the inside. It was a bit weird, and I really felt overwhelmed with concern for my health. I continued with the line. I reached the front of the casket. I looked inside and I just stood there for a few seconds. In my mind, I whispered a prayer. I thanked God for allowing me to know her as my cousin and I was sorry that my cousins, Kelly and Chrystal, and her granddaughter Robin will have to manage without her. I turned and walked back to my spot in line as we passed the first row of close family members pausing to hug whoever needed one. I noticed who could have been, Chrystal, my oldest cousin. She had her face buried into someone's shoulder, so I didn't see her good. As I continued to the next person, it was Chrystal's daughter Robin, who was practically raised by Cousin Daisy. I hadn't seen her since she was small. I hugged her and it reminded of the bond we shared decades ago. Then I hugged Kelly, the youngest daughter who stood next to her on the front row. I proceeded down the front row, and I passed Mommy and Tab. They didn't hug me. I kept walking until I reached a seat in the back of the sanctuary.

As soon as I sat down, I was handed an obituary. It was beautifully filled with amazing photos of Cousin Daisy's life. I skimmed through it and focused my attention on the final words. The services ended and I stood as the room cleared out beginning with the casket and then the front rows one by one to the back rows of the room. When I got into the lobby, I saw my cousins again. This time we were able to snap a few pictures and hug a little more. I didn't go to the repass because I still felt that my attire wasn't appropriate for the gathering, and I was still seeing the opportunity to earn more money driving Lyft. I grabbed up my copy of the obituary and hopped back on the road for a few hours.

A week later, I was at home in my empty 3-bedroom townhome and decided to light the grill for dinner. I called Pink and Jr and invited them over. Caveman and Cason were already in the area. It was beginning to look like a normal late afternoon for all of us. My phone rang and I looked at it with surprise and concern because it was China and she literally never called me. I answered and all I could hear was her frantically crying and yelling something about Mommy. I told her to calm down and tell me what is going on. China told me that Mommy had just confessed the unthinkable to her. I was on **PINS AND NEEDLES** waiting for her to spit it out!

She finally says, "Girl, Mommy just told me that Daddy is not my real father!" For a split second my whole life froze. I was stuck in disbelief. My disbelief wasn't about Mommy finally telling China the truth, but disbelief that she held a lie like that for our entire life! It wasn't until that moment that I realized something that I never imagined. Mommy could tell a lie. I mean a real intentional lie! In that moment, I realized that all my unanswered questions were suddenly valid. I snapped out of it and told China to come over right away so that we could talk more. Once I hung up the phone from her, Pink, who was next to me the whole time, looked at me and asked what was that about? I told her the news that I had just heard from China. She couldn't believe it.

My next thought was, how is that even possible? China is the 2nd oldest born after Roy. I am the one who's always had questions about my existence. I am the one who doesn't have any baby pictures. This doesn't make sense.

China arrived at my house. We arranged ourselves in my office created by me, in the back of the house off from the kitchen. China sat down and began to tell me the details of the story. Turns out that China needed a copy of her birth certificate from the dept of Vital Records, and without clear reason, she was told that her record could not be found with the information she was providing. She was instructed to go get her mother for further verification.

She went on to say that she contacted Mommy and let her know that she was going to pick her up so that she could accompany her to the Department of Vital Records and retrieve her birth certificate. As they approached the Department of Vital Records building, China says that Mommy suddenly blurts out that the information that is on her birth certificate is correct. And after all of these years, turns out that Daddy is not her real father.

I could not believe my ears!

I said to China, "if what you're saying is true, then I know he can't be my dad either!"

It is no secret that I experienced a lot of traumatic situations over the years involving both of my parents. I was well out of tears by the time Daddy passed. They would often join forces with regards to me.

I told Pink to go grab my original birth certificate. I still had it after all these years, it had tape on the creases, but otherwise still intact. I kept it in a shoe box along with a bunch of old photos. My daughter grabbed the whole box and sat it down on the desk. As I popped the box opened, I begin to say that my birth certificate is still the original one from the year of my birth.

There it was, my original document that I had kept in immaculate condition for over 5 decades, presenting it as verification at school, courthouse, driving services and credit situations. I whipped it out and begin to look it over. I never noticed that the heading of the document did not read Birth Certificate, but instead it read Registration of Birth. I was confused. I continued to read the document. The next thing I noticed was that there weren't any parents listed. In fact, there were no details listed about my birth at all. Just my name and date of birth. No weight, time, length, location of birth, no NOTHING!

For the first time in my life, I realized that I didn't have an actual birth certificate. The questions swirled! Why would I not have a birth certificate? I am the last born of four children from a married couple. Where is my birth certificate? Everyone else had one. From the inside looking out I saw myself when we were kids, admiring all the artifacts, from birth certificates, footprints inked onto fancy paper, baby pictures, and memories of the beginning, experiencing the same exact feeling in that moment. Why did I get a registration? What happened to the rest of my story? It became more unsettling than ever before.

Pink and I began to google the document. According to Google, up until 1972, the document served as the official document used in leu of an actual birth certificate when information was missing from the application. China was confused too. We called Cousin Lia who is the daughter of Mommy's youngest sister, Judy. She practically lived with us her whole upbringing because her mother is Mommy's baby sister. We told her the news and shockingly, she already knew! She said that they all always knew that Daddy wasn't China's real father. This left us completely baffled and all I saw was wooden nickels floating around. China was devastated.

We moved on to the registration. Cousin Lia said that she had the same document. I was intrigued to find out why. I told her what Google said regarding the document.

She said, "Yes, that makes sense because some information was left off the hospital forms when I was born."

I was floored! I said, "What do you mean?"

She went to explain how Auntie Judy delivered her and left a blank space instead of her father's name on the application. She had the same document, and she didn't get her actual birth certificate until recent. My mind was racing with all sorts of questions. I had never been this close to answers, and I didn't know if after all this time I would be able to accept whatever was in store, but I still wanted them.

Chapter 25 Know

Now I needed to call Mommy because only she can let me know what information could have possibly been missing. I called and I asked her that very question.

I asked, "Mommy, why do I have a registration of birth instead of an actual birth certificate?"

Her voice pieced through the phone, "I ain't answering no questions about nothing!"

I said," Huh?"

"Mommy, I'm just trying to understand what's going on."

She was very frustrated, and yelled, "If you want to know something, go ask Tab!"

Tab is her mother and my grandmother. As instructed, I called Tab. Tab was over 90 years old and sharp as a razor, still retelling choice things from her childhood. I told her the situation and explained that I was looking for answers again. I had these same questions my whole life.

I felt that something will finally make since. Tab chuckled at first, then she told me about a man. She started the conversation off with saying that Daddy was not the father of any of us girls. She said that every time Mommy got pregnant, Daddy was locked up. I couldn't believe what I was hearing. Although I had my doubts about Daddy, deep down inside, it didn't feel that was it.

Tab went on to describe a light complected man, shorter than average height, with a big but on him. She said that he looked a lot like me, and he worked as a carpenter. She said Mommy broke his heart by choosing Daddy every time he got out of jail. I was shaking! We sat there in disbelief. China was speechless. We continued to sypher through the box of photos. I said, "that can't be right." I just could not see Daddy accepting that same situation repeatedly. He was not that type of guy.

We called Mommy again. This time, I told her what Tab had just said to me. Mommy became extremely angry.

She said, "Tab is lying, and if I wanted to believe her, then go on and don't call me again!" "Daddy is your father!"

She hung up the phone. I felt so bad in that moment, but oddly, she reminded me of me after getting caught in a lie. There, I said it. In that moment, I knew that Mommy was hiding something. As we sat there in disbelief, we begin to process different scenarios of what could be going on.

Several months had passed and Mommy continued to not talk to me. I continued to pay her cell phone bill each month, and she still never called. I didn't call her either because I just didn't know what to say. I felt that I had overstep her boundaries. I continued to support China with her discovery of half siblings and more family members from her biological father's side. I was at war between truth and lies in my mind, and I could only talk to God about it. I wanted to believe that this was the reason for the disaccord among us, but it didn't make sense to me. China's discovery only revealed new family dynamics that I had never explored before that moment. I literally could have been bought with a wooden nickel when I found out that China was only my half-sister. China didn't like Daddy at no point in our lives. I assumed she was older and had strict rules that I was too young to understand. Turns out, Daddy was aware of China's real dad, but Mommy was his wife. So Daddy was the only Daddy she ever knew.

Another afternoon during our now normal information sessions, my daughter came up with the only logical explanation to this.

She said, "you know, you don't look like anyone in the immediate family; You look like family, but not immediate family."

I said, "I know that. That's always been clear to me."

She then said, "Maybe you're asking the wrong questions."

I asked, "How so?"

She continued to say, "Well, I don't think Grandma is not going to lie today about stuff. She'll avoid the question first. She said Daddy is your father because he is."

"You never asked if she was your mother."

Suddenly a weird sensation like I have never felt in my entire life zipped up my spine and lingered for a few seconds. I was stuck.

China threw her head back in laughter, saying, "girl, stop playing."

But Pink wasn't laughing at all, and neither was I. Pink went on to say that the only person in the family that I resembled more than anyone is Cousin Daisy, who we had just attended funeral services for a few weeks earlier. In an instant, I shuffled through the box of old photos again and discovered a few pictures of her. I found a few photos of her and her two daughters, and a few of her and her granddaughter. I must agree with my daughter on this one, we sure do look a lot alike. Every feature was an exact match.

I thought, wow, why is this so, and how come I never noticed this before? I thought maybe she noticed and that explains the way she used to look at me, with wonder in her eyes. The more I explored Cousin Daisy's life, the more I realized that we had a closer connection than I had been led to believe.

Later that night, when I was alone, I prayed for answers and clarity. I cried myself to sleep and had the most lucid dreams ever imagined. What if it's true, I felt betrayed and played with my whole life. I felt disrespected on levels I didn't have words for. I felt that for all these years Mommy really meant that I was a problem. Oh God, that would mean her love for me could have been tainted. I felt like a victim, like my real identity was stolen away from me since birth. They literally allowed me to struggle trying to be who they told me I was, instead of what God created me to be. At what point, do I get to know my truth? I struggled to please her and to fit in with my siblings for years. I was told that I was different by anyone and everyone who encountered our family. I thought about how Mommy led China to believe Daddy was her father knowing the truth and when I asked her why she did that, she replied, "It is not your business!" To this day though? We are adults now with families of our own, it's not fair to keep the truth from us. Then I thought, if Mommy could allow China to live her whole life under that lie, why would she not do the same thing when it comes to me?

When I woke up, I was still exhausted from the battle in my mind. I didn't have anyone to call. I prayed more and went on with my day. The family started weighing in. Cousin Scoop, Roy, and Cousin Lia were on board to find out the truth. We all agreed that something was wrong. They had questions and answers. I could never explain to anyone how this possibility was affecting me because everyone began to become concerned about Mommy's capacity to take this news. We had countless conversations over the phone and put all kinds of stories together. We were calling on other family members for answers and things were starting to come together.

We discovered that during the time of my birth, my family was very close knit. Mommy and Daddy were neighbors as teens. Cousin Daisy relocated from the South with Chrystal and Kelly and moved in with Tab to start a new life. At that time, Mommy had Roy, China, and baby Risha. Daddy's family lived right across the grass from them. They were all very close. We looked at many pictures of them from decades ago and we all saw ourselves in our parents. I had so many questions. I began to ask about my baby picture again. It's been years since I searched. We all decided to meet up at Tab's house one day because she was and always will forever be the gatekeeper of all family archives.

Tab was so happy to have us hang out with her all that day. We looked through thousands of pictures of so many family members, but still not one picture of me as a baby. I left there knowing that I was on to something, and I accepted that in God's time, the truth would be revealed to me. I continued to pray. I wanted to find balance in all of this, and I spent months considering how discovering my truth would affect others. I became overwhelmed with feelings and thoughts of how this could have happened. The big question for me was if Mommy wasn't my birth mother, then who was?

Chapter 26 Just Peachy

During the time of no contact, Mommy communicated through close family members. She heard that I was still asking questions. At the same time, Pink and I were making plans to take a huge leap of faith and relocate to Georgia to start new lives. I always wanted to live down South. I visualized purchasing a large piece of property and building a home big enough for me, my grown kids, and all my grandkids to live in comfortably. I researched employment opportunities and started applying for upcoming openings. I made a few trips and did some touring around and I participated in interviews remotely. I was offered a position and I accepted. Next, I researched housing in the area where my school was located. I narrowed choices down by considering only communities that were within a 10-mile radius from my work location. I selected an apartment in Gwinnett County Georgia. Plans were set and I was scheduled to relocate at the end of June.

I had about sixty days to make my move. Pink's plans were delayed, and she wouldn't be able to go so soon. I had to go ahead of her and start my job there. Before I moved to Georgia, Mommy and I had a conversation. I asked her about my birth certificate again. She casually told me that she left the hospital sedated and she forgot to get it. I asked her if she recalled the hospital, I was born in. She told me that she couldn't remember. I asked her about my baby picture, and she became annoyed. She flipped out and begin yelling.

She yelled, "So, you think I'm just some dummy that's going to take care of somebody's else's baby!?"

She then said, "I did all the work! I put in the time!"

"If you want somebody else to be your mother than you go right ahead!" "I should sue you for all the money I spent!"

I couldn't believe what I was hearing again. I didn't recognize her in that moment. From the inside looking out, she was looking at me but yelling at Daddy. All I could think about in that moment was wooden nickels. She never mentioned how she carried me for nine months or went through hours of labor. Never. I was stunned. I wondered what point triggered the switch. I felt like I was nine years old again.

I took the blame. I started feeling that I was disrespecting her by questioning her. I had no right to wonder. Suppose I'm waay off. I could be wrong. I begin to pray for forgiveness. I prayed that this inquiry into my origin is meant for me to know and that alone is the guiding force behind it, not anything else. I don't want to inflict pain on anyone by unintentionally exposing something about their life because it is directly connected to my story. I could not get pass the wonder. I didn't know who I was anymore. I struggled every day at work, and I lacked a solid support system. All I had was my prayers to guide me through.

In the summer of 2019, I moved to Georgia alone. I was a completely lost soul. I was buried under decades of pain, confusion, and hope. I realized that I had to meet me. I learned that I had no idea who I was as a person. I spent my entire life trying to please people and figure out why I was never quite enough for anyone in every single relationship, friendship, or the like; to include relationships with siblings and parents. I kept having flashbacks that reminded me and confirmed how I ended up here. Hard to understand and believe even now. I remember going to the hair salon as a kid with a full healthy head of hair and to have it cut off to a small afro with a jerry curl so that I could look like my sister whose hair texture was completely different from mines. TRAUMA... I couldn't stop crying. Never being seen. Always suppressed. I prayed for healing.

Lucky for me, my apartment was amazing. Much better than any I'd seen in Baltimore. The property was gated, and had a pool, tennis court, golf course, pet park, picnic area, playground, and much more. The rent was $1350.00 plus utilities. I had two bedrooms and two full baths in the roommate style floorplan. In unit laundry, kitchen, separate dining area, living room, and a sunroom. It was huge too. I had the ground level unit on the front of the building, and I was able to park my car directly in front of my apartment. It was perfect!

Several months had passed and I was still adjusting to my new life in Georgia. It was the best thing that I could have done at that time. I excelled in my teaching career and started getting familiar with my immediate neighbors. I was blessed to have a building full of working professionals. I worked a part time job at the local grocery store in the bakery department to help me get familiar with the people and the culture of my immediate surroundings. God was my tour guide.

I had one friend nearby who I'd met virtually when I still lived in Baltimore. He was originally from Baltimore, and we had a lot of mutual friends. We talked regularly over the phone when I still lived in Baltimore, we visited one another a few times before I made the move to Georgia. We bonded on the strength of his father being good friends with Roy. His father taught me how to cut my son's hair when they were kids. I knew his dad well. He knew my dad too. He told me that he remembered stories about my dad robbing the dice games around Strawberry Hill back in the day. I didn't know anything about that. He had been living in Georgia for a few years, and he had information like where to find the best seafood in the area.

When I became a permanent resident of Georgia, we saw one another regularly but we never committed to being in a relationship. LB didn't think he was on the up and up. Our apartments were only a 10-minute drive apart. So we were like old neighbors, borrowing toilet paper and exchanging recipes. We spent all our spare time together. Conversations would range from religion to politics with Strawberry Hill in the middle. I assisted him with interview techniques and helped him land a stable job in his career field. We listed one another as emergency contacts for employment records. We were friends. He was the only person that I associated with on a personal level in the entire state of Georgia, and he knew that. From the inside looking out, that was what made our friendship special. As soon as I got comfortable enough to tell LB that she was wrong about him, I got a reality check.

Time went on, he started to become unavailable due his busy work schedule. I already knew that I should prepare to be amazed, so I prayed about it. A few weeks had passed, and I hadn't heard anything from him. I remember praying for his wellbeing. Then one day, I scrolled through IG and saw a video that he posted of him and his family hanging out in another City. He had a wife and a big kid. He looked very happy. I was relieved to see that he was well, but I was hurt, and I felt abandoned yet again. I had been through enough heartache, and I knew how to deal with this one *expeditiously*. I sent him a text that read, "I forgive you, because I know that God used me to TEACH you what love is, and he used you to TEACH me what love is not." I never contacted him again. I didn't appreciate what he said about Daddy anyway.

I found joy in teaching and stayed involved with school activities. My fifth graders completed an entire school year virtually and made huge academic gains. They graduated by way of a drive by parade with their names spray painted on staff member's cars. We held a virtual ceremony and emailed diplomas to the students. If they wanted an actual copy, we expected them to print one out. The pandemic allowed me to really see things from a different perspective. I felt like my world as I had always known it to be, was about to change somehow in a major way.

A few months had passed by before I knew it. I barely talked to LB and Cousin Tricie on the phone for hours almost every day like we used to. I worked my normal school day, the after-school program, and tutored online in the evenings. I continued to work at the bakery and drive for Uber and Lyft on the weekends to gain knowledge of the land. My finances were in order, and I was thinking about purchasing my first home. I was busy with writing lessons, maintaining my weight, and praying that God continues to guide my steps. LB and I would fall asleep without ever hanging up. When I wasn't working, I told her every detail of my days. We face timed when I shopped, drove to work, or cooked in my kitchen. I didn't want to get into meeting new people especially after whatshisface. I talked to God regularly. I had my new life as a single empty nester living alone in a new State, with no friends, and my 50th birthday was approaching.

For my 50th birthday, LB and Cousin Tricie were both coming to visit me in Georgia for the first time since I'd moved. It had been a year and a half since I left Baltimore. I was so excited to see them both. I planned everything for the whole week that they were going to be there. LB's flight came in a few hours before Cousin Tricie's. Pink and some more guest arrived by car. The party wasn't starting until later that night, so we had the whole day to catch up. We did some shopping and cooking before prepping for the big event. I celebrated my 50th birthday surrounded by people I loved in my new hometown. God had already made my birthday all that I prayed for. We had a time! Before they all left to return home to Baltimore, I already had plans in place to join them for the holidays.

Three months later I went to the Baltimore for the holiday break, and homesickness smacked me in the face. It was the first time that I saw everyone since my birthday. I felt like a tourist. We hung out like old times. The break went by quick and returning home to Georgia was tougher than it had ever been. I was missing everyone before I crossed the first state line.

I focused on work and recovering to normal life after the pandemic. I was still in a strange land with a lot to learn. I no longer worked from home and my hour long each way commute was added to my daily routine. I became occupied with work so much, my interactions with friends and family members slowed down. It had gotten to the point where I could only rely on long holiday breaks for visits. It had been several weeks since I had facetime conversations with anyone.

Chapter 27 Ladybug

One early Saturday morning LB called me, for the first time in a long time, and I immediately got excited. I was thinking she was going to tell me that she was busy with work too, and that's the reason why I hadn't heard from her. I answered the phone and she said, "Hey girl. I been calling you and calling you, but you weren't answering." I said, "LB, I haven't received any calls from you." She said, "oh" and rambled on. She asked about the whatshisface guy that I hadn't heard from in months. I reminded her of that, and she said, "oh" again. We went for a few minutes and the call dropped. I assumed she was multitasking at the time, and she would call me back soon. But she didn't. I went on with my normal routines. LB stayed on my mind. I reminisced on how we called ourselves the golden girls and how we would have phone call conversations like that ever since we were kids. That feeling made me smile that whole day.

On Monday I went to work and while I was on hall duty, I got a notification on my phone that I had never received before. It said that a pair of EarPods was trying to connect to my handset. I was confused because I didn't own any EarPods. The notification bothered me a little, but I didn't give it too much thought. I finished hallway duty after a few minutes and went to my classroom.

Before any of my students arrived, my phone rang. I looked and it was a number with a Baltimore area code. I knew it was important because anyone who knew me, knew when to call me. I answered the phone, and it was LB's son. He called to tell me that he had just found LB in her house unresponsive. She was gone.

Without ever moving the phone from my ear, I grabbed my keys and ran to my car. I went home packed a few essentials and hopped on the road. I didn't bother to check for gas. All I wanted to do was get to Baltimore as fast as I could to help her. I didn't know what I was experiencing. LB's sudden passing almost took me out, but my faith in God renewed my strength. I am so grateful that we were best friends till the end just we always said. I wrote this poem for her:

Ladybug & Butterfly

I don't how I feel...
I don't know what to say.
I pray for strength and understanding.
To guide me through each day.

I lost my lifelong best friend.
My sister in every way.
With the spirit of a Ladybug
Man up, is what she'd say!

She'd remind me of my strength.
~She admired it so much.
She would tell me to keep it moving.
Especially when things get rough.

The loving memories within me,
only allow me to seem unchanged.
That's the beautiful work of Ladybug,
Protecting Butterfly's broken wings!

After LB's passing, I was left with an emptiness that I had never experienced before. I struggled every day and lost sleep most nights. My weight dropped down to 169 pounds; I could fit into a size 10 in pants. I hadn't worn a size 10 since I was 10 years old. I didn't have anyone to talk to so, I stayed talking to God.

One day, he spoke back! I received a direct message notification on my phone one evening. I was having a real hard time all week long. Struggling and feeling defeated. My faith was being tested. The message was from a guy from Strawberry Hill who I had known of since elementary school. While growing up we never communicated at all, but I could pick him out of a crowd. We were friends on social media only and we didn't interact there either, so I was surprised to receive a message from him. I opened the message, and it was a sermon from the church he attended. I had never heard of the church, but it was a big church in Baltimore. I listened to the sermon, and I was absolutely blown away by what I heard. I played it over and over a few more times. Each time, I heard something else that I had missed the time before. The message was literally for me.

Chapter 28 The Message

  I was laying across the couch in my dark living room. The only light on came from the stove that I treated like it was a night light for the apartment. I was talking to God, I grabbed my phone and decided to listen to the sermon. At first, I listened to what felt like 30 minutes of hymns sung by the choir. I sat the phone down so I could just relax and listen. The pastor's voice started, and I glanced at my phone to see what he looked like. I put the phone back down on the coffee table in front of me, an arm's reach away. Turned over and nestled back into my comfortable spot with the sermon playing. The pastor was speaking from 1 Peter chapter 2 verses 9 - 10 of the message translation versions, He quoted the text,
"But you are the ones chosen by God. Chosen for the high calling of priestly work. Chosen to be a holy people, God's instruments to do his work and speak out for him to tell others of the night and day difference he made for you - from nothing to something, from rejected to accepted."
~ 1 Peter 2: 9 - 10
I picked my phone back up and sat up on my couch.
He began the sermon by saying, "You are the one."
"There is something that I need to tell you that you need to know about you; There is something that you need to affirm about you."
He continued along those lines, and I was at full attention waiting to learn what the thing was.
Then he said, "God chose you."
He went on to explain exactly what he meant.
He continued with, "God chose you to be his voice, his ears, his heartbeat to his people. God has chosen you to represent him as a spiritual presence in a natural world."

Then he said, "Peter writes this letter 1 Peter verse 1 to persons identified as the chosen strangers."

"Persons who had first-hand experience with the power of God. Persons who have been endowed with the spirit of God. Persons, *'Cherry'* who have been gifted to be the visible and active God experience to this world."
I jumped up from the couch, grabbed my phone charger, and went over to my desk. He continued to PREACH! It felt like God was in my apartment telling me this message himself.

Especially when he said, "Get ready for a future that makes yesterday make sense today."
He said, "you must walk unapologetically in your purpose."

It was confirmation! I needed to continue seeking answers.

In the fall of 2022, China and I decided to discreetly take a sibling DNA test. China agreed to the test. We figured that since Daddy was confirmed not to be her father, but Mommy is her mother, we should be half-sisters if Mommy is my mother too. I ordered the DNA kits and had them shipped to China's house in Baltimore and I drove up from Georgia over the Thanksgiving break to take the test with her. We followed the instructions and mailed in our samples.

I returned home to Georgia and waited weeks for the results. It was pain staking! I made notes, studied old photos, and checked for updates every day. Mommy stood her ground, and everyone started judging me. Mommy was telling my children and other family members that I was crazy and attention seeking for stirring up family drama. She even ordered a copy of my birth certificate from the Department of Vital Records and had my grandson text me a copy of it.

The text came through my phone so randomly and unexpected. Mommy and I hadn't spoken in months. I asked my grandson why did I receive the text? He said, he didn't know, and that one-day Mommy just asked him to send it to me. I printed it out, looked it over, and placed it in my desk drawer. I didn't feel that it would help me answer any questions because it was just the generic copy the Department of Vital Records provided to people for general purposes. I ordered the same copy back in 2018 when this whole thing started. The copy has Mommy and Daddy listed as my parents. It also has my birthweight. Once I received the message, Mommy called and asked me if that satisfied my curiosity. I said yes, and I mentioned that I had a copy before this one.
She asked, "What does yours say?"

I was confused again. "What do you mean, what does mines say, it says the same thing that yours say."

She said, "OKAY" and ended the call. I thought the whole interaction was strange especially because her tone was filled with uncertainty. I grabbed my safe and dug out the copy of the birth certificate that I ordered back in 2018. I grabbed the copy she sent and placed them side by side. At first, they looked identical. I started down the documents line by line when I noticed something strange. Now considering that these documents were ordered four years apart, and formats change over time, I wondered why both documents were consistent where it required the legal name of my mother at the time of my birth. On the document sent by her in 2022, the line was blank. On my copy ordered in 2018, the line was blank as well. This startled me because I am the last born of four children to a married couple. So, I know for a fact that the legal name of my mother at the time of my birth should clearly read <u>Mommy Heal</u>. But it didn't. The space was blank.

    I called the department of Vital Records in Baltimore to find out why would the line be left blank. I was not ready for what I was told by the clerk on the other end of the phone. Once I reached the correct department, I connected with a lady who asked me a few questions and then placed me on hold. When she returned to the phone she asked me basic identification questions like my name, date of birth, and name of my parents. She placed me on another brief hold. She came back to the phone and asked me what I was looking for specifically. I explained to her that on the copy of my birth certificate, line *7a: Legal name of child's mother at the time of child's birth*, is blank, please tell me why.

She said, "Well that's not a normal thing. When people are adopted, certain things are left out of the copy for privacy reasons."

I said, "What?" She continued, "umm, let me see here."
She said she had my document right in front of her on the screen and she could see the blank line. She placed me on hold again. She returned to the phone this time; she was a bit apprehensive with her responses. She told me that I would need to make an appointment to come in and request a record review. I would be able to see my original birth record.

I made that appointment for the next available date which was several weeks out. I begin to research information on adoption laws in Maryland during my birth year. I learned that there were an entire community of adults born in that same era with similar situations. They formed several different groups to help search and support one another in obtaining information about their natural birth parents. I read blogs, watched interviews, and journaled while waiting for my appointment.

The communication from Baltimore faded a bit, and I hardly had conversations with anyone for a while. Finally, the Sibling DNA test results came in. I saw the notification and immediately broke out into a sweat. I was at work when the email arrived. I waited until I got home to read it. I had to prepare for the news physically, mentally, and spiritually. I got home, placed my things down, kicked off my shoes, put on a cup of coffee, and then I went up to my room to change into something comfortable. I returned to the kitchen to grab my coffee that was now piping hot. I fixed it up and went back to my room. It's time. I was so nervous. I prayed first and then I sat down at my desk and opened my laptop.

I took a deep breath, and I clicked on the email. It was four pages long. At first glance, it was a lot of information. I enlarged the page and clicked print. I still hadn't read any of the results yet. I'm just seeing words and numbers. I sip my coffee and place the cup down and click to open the document as a PDF. Okay, so now I can see the first page in full 8 x 10 view.

The first paragraph explained what was included in the four-page result, and how to determine the result using the data provided. I thought now, I am a professional educator and I hold two advanced degrees, this can't be too difficult. I continued reading. The next page, displayed the list of chromosomes tested and the amount shared between China and I. At the bottom of the page, a summary of the data points were displayed. I looked over the columns unsure of exactly what I was looking for. I just compared the numbers looking for matches and patterns. I didn't notice anything. I went back to page one and reviewed the section about what the chart represents. It was the sibling index values for full and half siblings side by side and compared. The paragraph read:

The probability of relatedness as full siblings is 44.9% as compared to an untested, unrelated random individual. The full sibling index is 0.81.

The probability of relatedness as half siblings is 92.6% as compared to an untested, unrelated random individual. The half sibling index is 12.56. The likelihood that the individuals are related as half siblings is 12.56 to 1.

I went back to the chart. I skimmed down to the bottom of the page, and I saw the two index values, again it read: COMBINED SIBSHIP INDEX (FULL-SIBLING): 0.81, PROBABILITY: 44.9%

COMBINED SIBSHIP INDEX (HALF-SIBLING): 12.56, PROBABILITY: 92.6%

So, I thought okay, we're half siblings because our sibship index 92.6%. I called China with the news. I said the result are in and we are half-sisters.

China said, "now you owe Mommy an apology."

I said, "okay" and we hung up the phone.

I felt an uncalming relief and I attempted to get up from my chair. I got extremely dizzy, and I fell into my clothes drying rack that stood near my desk. I was able to catch my balance as my granddaughter entered my room.

She said Grandma, "are you okay."

I said yes, "I think I just fainted."

She ran to get me a cold drink of water. I was sweating profusely. I laid across my bed and took some slow breathes. I prayed and drank the cold water. After a few minutes, I regained myself.

I said, "God, what was that?"

I returned to my desk, only to realize that I didn't read the entire email. Page three of the email contained the Results Interpretation Procedures, and page four contained examples and the Kinship Index chart. I thought, wait, there's a procedure? It read:

Are the individuals full or half siblings?

If a sibling pair would like to determine whether they are more likely to be full siblings or half siblings, the full sibling index value can be compared against the half sibling index value. If the full sibling index value is greater than the half sibling index value, then the individuals are more likely to be full siblings. If the half sibling index value is greater than the full sibling index value, then the individuals are more likely to be half siblings.

WOODEN NICKELS, The Inside Looking Out

I went back to the Sibship Index on the first page of the report. I saw the two values and did the math. According to the interpretation procedures, I compared the two values by using the formula and the examples provided: If a sibling pair has a full sibling index value of 100 and a half sibling index value of 2, then they are more likely to be full siblings than half siblings (because the full sibling index value is greater than the half sibling index value). A comparison of the full sibling index value versus the half sibling index value (100 ÷ 2 = 50) indicates that in this example, the full sibling index value is 50 times greater than the half sibling index value. If the full sibling index value is 50 times greater than the half sibling index value, it suggests that the sibling pair is 50 times more likely to be full siblings than half siblings. As another example, if the half sibling index value is 20 and the full sibling index value is 1.5, then the sibling pair is more likely to be half siblings than full siblings (because the half sibling index value is greater than the full sibling index value). A comparison of the half sibling index value versus the full sibling index value (20 ÷ 1.5 = 13.33) indicates that in this example, the half sibling index value is 13.33 times greater than the full sibling index value. If the half sibling index value is 13.33 times greater than the full sibling index value, it suggests that the sibling pair is 13.33 times more likely to be half siblings than full siblings.

China and I had a combined full sibling index of 0.81, and a combined half sibling index of 12.56. To compare and find the Kinship Index value, 12.56 is divided by 0.81. The result is 15.51. Based on these results, China and I could be related as half siblings, but we could also be related as cousins.
Recommended interpretations are as follows:

The genetic evidence is supportive of a full or 1/2 sibling relationship if the kinship index is greater than 10.
The genetic evidence is not supportive of a full or 1/2 sibling relationship if the kinship index is less than 0.1.
The genetic evidence is inconclusive of a full or 1/2 sibling relationship if the kinship index is 0.1 through 10.
Combined Kinship Indexes and their verbal equivalent:
Combined Kinship Index >10000 = Practically proven
Combined Kinship Index from >1000 to 10000 = Highly likely
Combined Kinship Index from >100 to 1000 = Very likely
Combined Kinship Index from >10 to 100 = Likely
Combined Kinship Index from >1 to 10 = Slightly more likely than unlikely
Combined Kinship Index of 1 = Inconclusive
Combined Kinship Index from 0.1 to <1 = Slightly more unlikely than likely

Part of me wanted to see confirmation that China and I were half-sisters, and all of this would be over. But I couldn't accept the results without more questions. I felt that if Mommy was the biological mother to both of us, we should have much higher numbers for probabilities of relationship. I researched meanings of the results and probabilities. Research of relationship charts as well as other tools infer that China, and I looked more like cousins according to our DNA results. I didn't know if I was trying to convince myself or was, I really taking a learner's stance and processing information without bias. Something just didn't seem right. I called China back to let her know what I was thinking, but it was too late. She had already called Mommy with the test results. Now Mommy believes that I am convinced that she is my birth mother. She knows for a fact that China does. China became agitated with me. She told me that I was making her pressure rise and she didn't want to talk about it anymore. She said she needed a nap and she'll call me tomorrow.

Before she hung up, she told me that Mommy found my original birth certificate and a few of my baby pictures. I said, "What?" "You're kidding me! Not after all these years. Did you see them?"

China said, "not yet but I'll send them to you tomorrow when I go to Mommy's house".

I said OKAY and let her rest. I couldn't stop thinking about what Mommy planned on sharing with China. I know for a fact that a picture of me as a baby has never been seen in my entire life. I remember countless occasions of me searching and hoping and praying to come across it someday.

I wanted to know what I looked like as an infant. I had only seen pictures of me from about the age of three and older. Mommy always claimed that I had plenty of pictures from my childhood, and she's right. But I was interested in the earlier ones. In fact, the first picture of me and Mommy together was when I was about three years old. It was an ongoing issue for me since I could remember. I never had an infant picture of myself. I couldn't participate in activities at work or school when it involved sharing a baby picture of myself. I could never see myself in my children as an infant because I didn't know what I looked like. I never knew which features I was born with, besides my birthmark. I never knew how much hair I was born with. I never knew my complexion at birth. I never knew my birthweight or place. I never knew who cut my cord, or who delivered me. Who was present when I was born. Who loved me? How can questions like these annoy my mother? They did, so I kept them to myself. After all, I wasn't included in the conversations Mommy and China were having behind the scenes. Mommy found out about the DNA test and suddenly, baby pictures and birth certificates appear. I felt bamboozled! I couldn't understand how China was being so easily convinced that I was imagining this whole thing.

Chapter 29 Broken Record

The next day finally came. I called China as soon as I thought she was awake. She didn't answer until I called in the late afternoon.

She answered her phone by saying, "I'm sending them now!"

My heart was racing. Then the notification came through in a text, three images. I clicked on the first image and my heart dropped. It was the picture that I had always known. I was close to three years old, wearing a red holiday looking romper, seated on a couch next to Mommy wearing a huge afro wig. Mommy had her hand placed on my leg, barley touching me, and I sat there holding on to a toy that I still remember to this day. I zoomed in on the picture, and I noticed that Mommy had a swollen lower lip and a tiny band aid on her nose. I was instantly reminded of the fights her Daddy had. I noticed a brown cardboard box on placed on the end table next to the sofa we sat on.

I owed myself a joke in that moment and thought to myself, "must have been my first day in, and those were my belongings".

I had to laugh at myself to lighten the mood. The next image was three children, I'd also always known. One boy standing in a doorway, it was Roy. Two girls, one standing behind a stroller and the other inside of the stroller. They were on a porch. The smallest of the three was in the stroller with a hood on her head looking directly into the camera. The other girl had her head turned away from the camera. Judging from the sizes of the girls alone, I could easily see that they were China and Risha. I wasn't on the picture at all! The final image was a replica of a birth certificate. It had huge baby footprints on it. It had my last name misspelled. Place of birth was not listed. It did not contain a seal, signature, nor date issued. It was a prop that people could get in the hospital's gift shop.
I thought, "How could she?"

    I called Risha and sent her the picture with the three children on it.

    I said, "who is this?"

    Risha without any hesitation said, "Me, China, and Roy."

    I said, "where are you in this picture?"

    Risha said, "in the stroller."

    I told her that Mommy was telling China that it's me in the stroller. Risha chuckled and said, girl you know Mommy's getting old. We both laughed and said our goodbyes.

    I called China back to let her know that I wasn't on the second picture, and I was not a baby on the first picture, and the birth certificate is a souvenir from a hospital gift shop. I asked her if she had even looked at this stuff before she sent it to me. She was frustrated again and made it clear that she was officially out of it! I was left with more questions than answers yet again.

I sent the images to a couple of close family members for them to weigh in. They fell over with laughter and disbelief. They couldn't believe Mommy was presenting me with these images as her proof of maternity. Deep down inside I was broken. Time went on and questions lingered. The holidays were approaching again. We decided to do more DNA testing. This time we decided to go with a popular DNA company because we wanted to test a few of us at the same time for comparison.
While in town for the holidays, Roy, Cousin Lia, and I all submitted DNA samples.

I also went to my appointment with the Department of Vital Records to review my original birth record. I arrived a few minutes early for the appointment, took a number, and then took a seat. I was called to the first window for an initial screening which included the reason for my visit.

I said, "I have an appointment to review my original birth record."

The clerk looked at me oddly and said, "hold on a second".

She returned a minute later and asked me for ID. I gave her my Georgia State issued driver's license. The clerk looked at the ID and ask me to hang on again as she disappeared from the counter. She came back and this time she had some news for me. She informed me that I would not be able to review my original birth record, however she can provide me a certified copy of it.

I said okay, thinking I can read, hand it over. She handed me a copy of my birth certificate and it was exactly like the two I already received in the mail.

I said, "umm excuse me ma'am, I would like to see the original records containing details of my birth."

The clerk looked at me with confused frustration and disappeared from the counter, without asking me to wait like before. After a few minutes, a different clerk appeared. She engaged with me in a subtle tone and empathetically explained that I would be receiving what is known as the long copy of my birth certificate today.

The expression on her face confirmed the information I had researched regarding adoption laws found on the Maryland General Assembly's website regarding this matter. In 1947, Maryland laws were enacted to protect the identity of biological parents. They did so in a very messed up way for adoptees. The adoption rules state that when a child is born and the parents choose adoption, they create a new birth certificate with new parents listed as the real birth parents. Meanwhile, the original birth record is sealed in a vault for 100 years. No one can access the original record until that time is up. When adjustments to the law were made, which allowed access via court order, my birth year was excluded from the bill. There are hundreds of birth records from the early 1970's that fell into this trap of never knowing the truth.

The clerk provided me with the "long copy" of my birth certificate. It contained a few more details than the previous copy. The information was photocopied into a template. All the text was handwritten. It had my birth weight and time of birth on it. That was new for information for me. It also listed Mommy and Daddy as my parents but even on the photocopy, Daddy's name had clearly been corrected. The document did not satisfy the question of authenticity for me. I hit a brick wall with this one.

Meanwhile, a plethora of scenarios loomed among us. My cousins and I would have group chats and video calls to compare information and ideas of what could be going on. For weeks different things kept coming to the light. Like the fact that Cousin Daisy worked for a judge for several years and they developed a very close personal relationship. According to Kelly's post, the two of them were like family. Also, how Cousin Daisy, Chrystal, and Kelly were once very close to us and we spent a lot of time together and then one day, something happened, and we didn't spend time together anymore. Mommy's siblings all agreed that a lot of things happened during the time of my birth including big family feuds. Tab would simply say people were just people back then. None of them dared to uncover details of the times. From the inside looking out, I think we're on to something here.

Chapter 30 Exhibit A

Then one day Cousin Lia sends me a photo of a baby girl.

I said, "Who is she?"

Cousin Lia said, "I don't know, but I know who she isn't."

I asked, "What do you mean?"

She went on to say, "It's posted on Kelly's page and the caption says that it's her beautiful mother when she was a baby".

I said, "no way."

"I have a picture of Cousin Daisy as a baby sitting on Kelly's grandmother's lap."

I was confused and I said, "besides this picture is not that old."

"It's from the late 60's or early 70's."

"Her mother's baby picture is clearly much older, as it should be since she was born in the late 40's."

"The photo paper was poorer quality compared to this one."

Cousin Lia agreed and said, "Who do you think she is?"

I said, "I don't know but I feel like I saw this picture before at some point in my life."

"I feel like I asked if it was me and my mother told me no it wasn't when I was very small."

I examined the photo more. I thank God for providing me with technology. I was able to zoom in on it and I noticed a small light spot located on the chin exactly where my birthmark is. I suddenly experienced chills all through my body. I dropped the phone. I stared out blankly while my mind raced around the idea that I just saw a picture of myself as a baby! My heart palpitations went berserk, and I still can't explain how I felt.

I grabbed my phone back up and examined the photo some more. The baby girl looked to be about 6 months old. In the photo, she is sitting up with a white stuffed toy puppy in her lap. She is wearing a springtime dress and no tights, just little bobby socks and shiny black shoes. The collar on her dress reflected the small spot on the chin, which caught my attention. The photo had lots of blemishes on it, and some were difficult to distinguish them from the light spots that I was born with. The baby's hair was beautiful. It was cold black and full of big curls. The photo was taken from an angle that showed the side of the baby's face with the light spots on it. The baby's facial expression was blank. She had huge bright almond shaped eyes, but they looked very sad or confused. I don't know but she just didn't look happy. She had huge cheeks and the cutest perky lips that looked drawn on, like Pink's did when she was born. She was very light complexed, but her ears were dark like Pink's too. Her face was perfect. I zoomed in to see her facial features and I was blown away! I saw all my children in that baby's eyes. I saw what looked like my natural hairline. I saw the bags under my eyes and the star in the corner of my eye. I noticed my big ears tinted dark with my birthmark perfectly placed inside the crease. The photo was in black in white, but I could see every detail of what MY baby picture could be! For just the hope, I was so grateful to have another prayer answered for me in this lifetime! I thought, if this is me, I was a beautiful baby. I would literally fall in love with me for the first time in my life.

    I called Mommy to share the news. She answered the phone with hesitation in her voice, we were still no contact. I said, "Hey check this out," and then I sent her the picture.

I said, "open the text that I just sent you."

She did and she said, "who is this?"

I said, "Mommy, zoom in."

I was super excited to hear her response. Then Mommy said the unthinkable.

She paused and said, "this is not you!"

I said, "Huh?"

She continues to say, "Ummm this looks like...I think this Aunt Heather's daughter Halee."

She paused again and then in a different tone she asked, "Where did you get this from?"

I couldn't breathe for a second.

Then I responded, "Cousin Lia sent it over because she saw it posted as Cousin Daisy on social media, and that's not who it is."

Mommy again said that it was her Aunt's Heather's daughter, Halee. I was crushed. How could this be? Crushed that either she didn't recognize me in the picture as a baby, or she really had no idea what I looked like as a baby. I thought maybe she's suffering from a lifelong case of postpartum depression that caused her to block out early memories of me. I never mentioned the picture to her again. I sent the picture to China next. Her reaction made my head spin! After she looked at it, she said, "Girl this ain't you." I said, "Why do you say that?" China said, "because you didn't look like that." I asked, "Well, what did I look like?" China paused and blurted out, "We don't know what you looked like when you were a baby!" Then she ended the call. Roy didn't recognize the baby either.

Everyone believed Mommy because after all, she would know her own baby. Right? Then one day after a few weeks had passed, Mommy texted me a message about the picture. It read, this is my cousin Daisy when she was a baby, it's in her obituary. I simply replied, thanks. I felt like an idiot. I prayed for answers. I questioned my sanity. I had no idea what I looked like as a baby so how could claim the picture. Maybe I was wrong. I printed a copy of the picture out and pinned it to my vision board for safe keeping. Mommy maintained her silence thereafter as if all was settled. I had more questions, but I knew not to look to her for answers. I also knew that she worried about the situation, but she refused to speak with me. She refused to speak to me about anything for several months.

I wanted to ask my cousin Kelly about the picture of who she's claiming to be her mom. I wondered where it was kept for all these years. Who does it belong to? Who had it taken? I wanted to know if she would let me see it in person. Part of me had doubts after Mommy's reaction to seeing the picture, and I was scared to claim it as me. I couldn't stop thinking about it, because I could see me, and I wondered if there was a note written on the back of it. Cousin Lia felt that it could be too sensitive for her and that I should wait until the DNA results came in before ruffling any more feathers. So instead, I asked a few other cousins. I started with Cousin Tricie on Daddy's side, because I know that if anyone could pick me out of a crowd of baby pictures, it's her! Just as I could do the same on her behalf.

I was reluctant at first only because I knew Cousin Tricie was under her Dr's care, but she was always in good spirits and very happy to hear from me. We texted regularly, but we hadn't talked for a while. I stayed busy in Georgia trying to adjust to life after losing LB. Cousin Tricie was under her dr's care receiving cancer treatments. I sent her the picture, and she identified me right away.

She said, "Awww, this is you for sure cuz, look at your thigh, you were born with them MFer's...

We both burst into laughter."

She said, "you still have those dimples in your elbows."

We chatted through a few more memories and then she wanted to get back to her resting. I felt so relieved after speaking with Cousin Tricie. I didn't realize how much time had passed since we last laughed like that. I looked forward to seeing her when the holidays rolled around. I headed up to Baltimore for my now annual road trip. Cousin Tricie's birthday was two days after Christmas. We had lunch one afternoon, but she declined to hang out like we normally would when I came in town. She was a lot smaller too. I spent the night at her apartment and celebrated her birthday with her. We played music and danced and sang and even played dress up like when we were kids. She enjoyed going through my suitcase. She cooked food and we talked and laughed until we both fell asleep. The next day I left and soon after, I returned home to Georgia. It was priceless, and I'm so grateful that the conversations happened. I didn't realize that would be the last time we got to laugh like that.

Chapter 31 I need you God.

Meanwhile, "The moment you've been waiting on", email came. This time, I was petrified! It was January 5th; I remember it well because I had recently returned home in Georgia after spending the holiday break in Baltimore. I received a telephone call with news that Cousin Tricie's condition had been updated and she had been hospitalized since the day that I left Baltimore. Her daughter called to tell me that she had been moved into hospice care. I froze, said a prayer, and packed my bags again. I called my mechanic because my engine light was on, and I needed to have my car serviced before another 10-hour long road trip. The mechanic told me not to worry and that my car was like me, strong enough to handle the trip.

I took a nap, and then I hit the road. With tears streaming down my face for most of the 10-hour ride, I stayed in prayer that God if is your will, please allow me just one more sleep over with my cousin in Jesus' name! I facetimed Cousin Tricie's daughter while she was in the hospital room with Cousin Tricie and I was able to speak to her. The medical staff had begun to sedate her, and she was losing some alertness. I said her name, and she looked into the camera at me with a slight smile on her face.

I said, "I love you Cousin, I'm on my way." "
Please don't you go nowhere Cousin, I'm coming, please don't go nowhere."

Her smile brightened and she gave me a thumbs up. She said, "I'm good cuz".

I arrived at the hospital a few hours later to find Cousin still alive. She popped her eyes opened as soon as she heard my voice. She cracked a smile and softly closed her eyes again. Then she heard my granddaughter's high pitch voice yelling,

"Hi Cousin Tricie, I love you".

She chuckled. Cousin Tricie loved kids. I took her hand and prayed that she was comfortable and at peace. I prayed that she trusts God through all things, including this. As the night went on, the room filled and emptied with friends and family members expressing their love and concern for Cousin Tricie. People brought flowers and cards, some dropped off food, and drinks. I napped periodically throughout the night. The next morning, I thanked God for allowing to spend another night with Cousin Tricie. When I looked over at her, she was resting peacefully. Her breathes were slow and steady, and she would occasionally flinch. I whispered to her that I would be right back. I got up to take a shower, but I had to go outside to my car where my bags remained. It was so cold that morning.

As I left the room heading to the elevators, I noticed the nurse quickly walking into Cousin Trice's now, free of guest, empty room. The nurse had a few syringes grasped in her hand. I thought to myself, she is giving Cousin Tricie another dose of that medicine. As I walked down the hallway, the floors started to feel like quicksand, and I struggled to get there. My mind was racing with terror. I got to my car and grabbed my bags and headed back into the hospital.

I ran into my niece along the way. She was heading up to Cousin Tricie's room too. I was glad because I was jumping in the shower, and I didn't want to leave Cousin Tricie alone anymore. I told my niece about the nurse, and she hurried up to Cousin Tricie's room. I quickly finished my shower and returned to Cousin Tricie's room. It was still early, and other close family members begin to return to the room as well.

Cousin Tricie only had one daughter and two granddaughters at the time. Her daughter and youngest granddaughter were there too. Conversations kicked up and everyone was distracted but I kept my eyes on Cousin Tricie lying there in that hospital bed transitioning away from this lifetime as we know it.

Suddenly, it happened. Cousin Tricie took her last breath. She was gone. The room was silent, and reality sat in. The screams were heart wrenching coming from the room. The nursing staff ran in, and they were in tears as well. Once everything settled down, we had to say our goodbyes, and leave the hospital. Everyone loved Cousin Tricie and she will always remain embedded in my heart.

I returned home to Georgia and waited on funeral arrangements. I was asked to write Cousin Tricies's obituary and to also provide a poem from the family. Her daughter provided me with the rough draft and wanted me to "fix it", but it was beyond fixing.

Then she went on to say, "Can you just please write the whole thing, but you have to leave your name out of it."

I was floored. How is that even possible? What are you asking of me? I was offended, hurt, confused, and devastated all at the same time. I couldn't talk to anyone about these feelings, but God! This child wants to literally erase me from her mother's life! This is crazy! Why? What did I do to offend her? I could only imagine how Cousin Tricie would feel.

Then I stopped. I stopped accepting the victim stance. I started thinking about how she must feel being the only child of Cousin Tricie and having to share her mother with someone else. She had every right to be selfish about her mother at this time. From the inside looking out, I never experienced the type of mother daughter love that they shared.

I complied without any further questions. I wrote a beautiful obituary and a poem. It was beautiful and I don't have an ounce of regret. The poem never made it to the obituary, but some guests were able to get a copy and Pink read it aloud during the remarks part of the service. I titled it, My Cousin Tricie.

My Cousin Tricie

My cousin Tricie was my first best friend.
Born 3 months apart, locked in since then!
We shared grandparents, aunties, uncles & friends.
Hopes, dreams, ideas & aspirations.
We dressed alike when we were kids,
We had sleepovers and shared the same bed.
We had parties and arguments like all cousins do.
When discipline was handed down, it came in two!
From Childhood fears, teenage years,
Weddings, divorces, kids, & grandkids.
I am so grateful to God for all the times we had...
The laughs, cries, good times, and bad.
I never thought I'd have to live a day,
With my cousin Tricie not just a phone call away.
My cousin Tricie was my first Best Friend!
I'm so blessed that God chose me to be her cousin.

It wasn't easy reaching that point in my thought process and actions. I called on an unsung hero and remembered the conversation that we had. A few weeks earlier, when I was in town and the DNA samples were submitted, I scheduled an appointment to speak with the Pastor who I had been following ever since I received that message he delivered while in Georgia. I started attending his online services from the day that I received the DM several months back.

Ironically, the appointment to meet with him, fell on the same day that Cousin Tricie passed away. I had forgot all about it until I received the notification as I was leaving the hospital. I had time to stop pass Pink's house, where I lodged whenever I came to town, to freshen up. The appointment was a zoom call, so I just needed to secure a good signal. My laptop would not connect to Pink's wifi so I had to run outside, hop in my car, and take the call using my cell phone. I joined the meeting. I was so nervous. I didn't know what to expect. I had never in my life had a one-on-one conversation with a pastor. I can count on one hand the number of times I stepped foot inside for services somewhere. I prayed that I refrain from using any cuss words. I took a deep breath and clicked camera on. He appeared after a few seconds. I wasn't sure if he was alone in the room, and I didn't know how this was going to go.

He said a bold and reassuring hello. I said, "Hi". I tried to smile but the tears came from somewhere and I struggled to get myself together. He looked confused but patient.

He said, "Let's pray".

He waited a few seconds and then he asked, "What brings you here?"

I told him about Cousin Tricie and my road trip, and from the look on his face, I could tell he thought that was the nature of my visit, but I continued to speak. I took another deep breath and explained my situation.

> I explained, "a few years ago, I received a message in my DM from a childhood friend, who across this lifetime, I've had little to zero interactions with."

"He is a member of your church, and he sent me one of your sermons."

"Before this, he never made any sort of contact with me. I'm not even sure how we became friends on social media."

"I watched the full video and experienced something unlike anything that I've ever experienced before!"

"You delivered to me a direct message from God."

"You said my name and you spoke on situations that I have been experiencing my whole life."

"If my faith was ever tested, this was it."

"In the message, you spoke from bible verse 1 Peter 2:8- 10."

I recalled what he said, "You have a story to tell, and your story is not just any story. It is proof that your life is a walking testimony of God's work. Your story is one for the others and You are the one God chose to tell it."
He was staring back at me with wonder in his eyes and it looked like he mouthed the words, "she's chosen", to someone in the room.

I continued to tell him about the DNA situation and that I needed answers. When I finished explaining to him my reason for being there, he said, "Wow". Then he asked me, okay so now what?

I replied, "I don't know, I'm here so I guess it's return to sender?"

We both laughed and the mood was lightened. He advised me to wait for all the answers that I needed and to not stray from my purpose. That's exactly what I did.

I attended Cousin Tricie's viewing and paid my respects. She looked beautiful and at peace. While there, I noticed the slide show of memories displayed on the big screen as soft music played. I felt like I was in some sort of twilight zone as I watched the accounts of Cousin Tricie's life from birth to passing display before my eyes. I noticed that I didn't appear in any of the pictures, and the memories displayed didn't include me. Even the senior prom picture where I was her date, had me cut off.

I spoke briefly with one of Daddy's sisters while there. I told her about the DNA testing and all. She seemed surprised to learn that the test confirmed that I was a Heal. It seemed like until that moment, I was like China in her eyes, not Daddy's child. I understood in that moment I was seeing their real feelings about me. I understood how my presence could have secretly been a problem for them too. I never felt more displaced. I did not attend the funeral the next day. I didn't feel the need, I had written the obituary, and viewed the slideshow. I felt that everything else served as an agenda for the people who didn't matter! I was at complete peace in knowing that Cousin Tricie and I shared a lifetime of unconditional love that any pair of cousins could ever hope for.

Chapter 32 Do Not Assume

I returned home from my extended stay in Baltimore. I could finally take a closer look at the DNA results. The results from this DNA company seemed a lot easier to understand at first. Then I started to notice some major differences between Roy and I, especially how the DNA said we were related to Cousin Lia. Cousin Lia should be our first cousin, because Mommy and her mother, Aunt Judy are sisters, and she was for Roy. But for me, she was my second cousin. How is this possible? Mommy and Aunt Judy are sisters. The trend continued with all the DNA matches that we had in common on Mommy's side of the family. We even recognized some of the names of close and distant cousins who showed as matches. We started to rule out some of the scenarios that we imagined.

Before the DNA results came in, we had all started to believe that Cousin Daisy would likely be identified my birth mother. We had almost convinced ourselves based on the stories we heard from people who knew them well. We realized that scenario couldn't be right because from Mommy's side of the family, I matched on an entirely different generational line according to the DNA results. The results also confirmed that Roy and I both descend from the same paternal line.

However, the matches from Daddy's side of the family correspond correctly and Roy and I are on the same generational line. That could only mean one thing. My birth mother and Roy's birth mother is not the same person. If this is a fact, my birth mother would have to be the daughter of one of Mommy's close cousins. I yelled out loud, "Really Daddy?

I could clearly see his image, shiny Black skin face with his big bright grin accented with a teardrop embedded gold side tooth, tongue hanging out, yelling with an exaggerated flat tone, "Jokes on you Jaaaaaaackkkkkk...". I shook my head thinking, Wooden Nickels! I was so distraught; I spent the next several days depressed beyond depression. I prayed and prayed for inner peace and understanding. Then I looked at that baby picture one day, I still had it pinned to the wall beneath my vision board, something about the look in her eyes incited a riot inside of me. From the inside looking out she said, I deserved to be loved, respected, and acknowledged. I am a human being, and it is not my job or responsibility to ensure that someone else's secrets stay safe. When does my existence matter to anyone. I deserve to know the truth and I should not have to tip toe around my own feelings to protect the feelings of people who obviously will never see me for who I am. It's simple, just tell me the truth.

I needed to know what was that thing that happened? It dawned on me that my birth did not bring joy to anyone. Based on the process of elimination, facts lead us to one of Mommy's cousin's daughters as my possible birth mother. The next question is which one is more likely to have secretly given birth to a baby fathered by her older cousin's husband? Who was around during the time of my conception and birth?

I remember basic family tales and early memories of time spent together. There was so many of us running around back then, and the families were very close. I could easily recall my oldest cousins, and we suspected one of them. Cousin Daisy kept them both away from the family since I was small. When I was growing up, I heard stories of the oldest being away doing great things. From the inside looking out, after she had her first child, she became off the scene and Cousin Daisy pretty much raised her granddaughter. She was the cutest little girl that I had ever seen. She had the longest hair that she could easily sit on. She was my friend and I often bragged about her because she was so cute and playful. We were about 10 years apart in age. Later, my cousin had a son. By the time he was born, they had stopped coming around all together, so I never got to meet him. When he was a teenager, we loss him to a senseless act of violence. I attended his funeral services. I still remember walking up to the house from my car and seeing my other cousins standing around the front of the house wearing t shirts with his picture on the front of it. He was so handsome, and he had a beautiful smile. Although I never established a bond with him, I was deeply saddened by his passing. So much that I was sort of surprised that it affected in a way. My cousin was beautiful as I could remember her. She was very light skinned with lots of hair. Her daughter has some daughters of her own too. Ironically enough, they all look a lot like all my own granddaughters. I thought then that they must be closer in relation than we have been led to believe. So much evidence pointed to her, but I didn't feel comfortable bringing this matter to her.

We had to move forward with next steps, so one night Pink and I called her daughter, Robin. I felt that she would be more approachable because she wasn't directly involved. We were all friends on social media, and she posted a lot of information about Cousin Daisy who was her grandmother, and who she loved very much because she practically raised her. We were very close when we were younger but as an adult, I felt like I was contacting a stranger. I had never actually spoken with her as an adult. That was the extent of our closeness, so the first few attempts to reach her were fails. We tried a few times and then we got through. The conversation started with greetings. After all, this was a second time that she's being confronted with this situation.

The first time was back in 2018, weeks after Cousin Daisy had passed on. It wasn't the best time to bring up past deeds. At that time, we didn't have a fraction of the information that we had now. We let her know about the DNA test and that so far, the results looked strange. We explained how the results were placing me on a different generational line than Roy and Cousin Lia. We were almost convinced that Mommy is not my birth mom. We need to know who could be. She agreed to take the test. I was elated! I purchased the kit for her. Cousin Lia also purchased a kit for Tab. The two of them joining our search would help clear up some things. We waited weeks for the kits to arrive. Then we had the samples collected and submitted. We waited several more weeks for the results to come.

Meanwhile, we explored records and documentation from ancestors on both sides of the family. We have a huge family. Mommy's side alone account for thousands of cousins. Tab is one of fifteen children, so her DNA results will have a big impact on this situation. We studied census records, military data, marriage and divorce records, wills, death certificates, and birth certificates, just to name a few of the resources provided on the DNA site. We decided to shift gears and do some exploration of Daddy's side while waiting on round three of DNA test results. Roy and I shared a very large amount of DNA and based on that; we were labeled full siblings. At the same time, Roy matched Cousin Lia as her first cousin while I matched Cousin Lia as her second cousin on Mommy's side of the family. Roy also had more DNA than me as compared to the other matches. We explored the ancestral lines starting with common ancestors. On Daddy's side of the family, it was his mother and father, our grandparents. I clicked on Daddy's father and the screen read, "no matches". I thought this is strange. Were's Roy? I then clicked on Daddy's mother. Then I was floored again.

The screen opened with my grandmother's name in a box with a line extended from it leading to another set of boxes below it. In that set of boxes, it read Daddy's name in one of them and in the of another box read potential uncle. Each of those boxes had lines extended from them as well. Below Daddy's name, my name was listed. But Roy's name was listed under the box that read potential uncle. I thought this must be a mistake. This is saying that on Daddy's side of the family, Roy and I are first cousins! Before that moment, I honestly didn't think about the possibility of Daddy not being my father. I accepted that he was my father since the discovery of Mommy being the parent in question.

I thought about my uncles. Daddy's two younger brothers. One was murdered in Strawberry Hill in 1973. I don't have any memories of him, I don't even know what he looks like. I was told that he died before I was born, but that was not true. I was three years old at the time of his death. It made me think about what could have happened to him. Could he be involved in this somehow? He had no known children nor wife according to his surviving sisters. I asked both of my aunts, his sisters, for pictures of him since I had never seen him. I never got the photos. Meanwhile, I used the resources available on the DNA website. I searched for information about his death, schools, and military. The DNA website had no records at all for him, like he never existed. I couldn't find an old newspaper article or anything. Not a trace of him anywhere. Until one day, a hint appeared on the DNA website. It was a record from the Social Security Administration. I couldn't help but wonder if he fathered a child and someone tried to collect financial support after his death. The record didn't have those details.

Chapter 33 Who said What

    Roy and I decided to visit one of Daddy's lifelong friends who I regard as my Godfather. He still lived in the old neighborhood, Strawberry Hill. When we were small, he lived across the country in California, so it was always a treat when he came to Baltimore for visits. He always came baring gifts, and it was always a party going on in his honor. He was Daddy's best friend. He was now in his mid-70's, and he hadn't seemed to have missed a beat. He looked great! Still sharp as a tack. He didn't look a day over 45. When Roy and I arrived at his house, he was overwhelmed. He was amazed at how we grew up. He was so happy to see Roy. He just kept telling him how much he resembled Daddy. He chuckled at times when Roy said certain things that reminded him of Daddy. He was so proud of me for completing graduate school, relocating to Georgia, and just surviving the hood! We talked about so many memories from back in the day.

    We got to the reason for our visit. We told him about the DNA testing and what we had discovered so far. We explained that we are almost convinced that Mommy was not my birth mom, and after the first few rounds of DNA testing, it's starting to look like Daddy could possibly be father to only one of us.

He was not confused at all. Initially, he laughed. Then he straightened up and begin to explain some things. He reminded us of who Daddy was and how he moved in the streets back then. He also reminded us about the level of loyalty Mommy always had for him. He told us that he is 100 precent sure that whatever Daddy presented to Mommy, she would be in full support of it. Anything! He went on to say that he could see Daddy bringing a baby home to Mommy and Mommy raising that baby as her own, because that is how tight they were. He said that he could also see Daddy taking what he perceived as his from whoever had possession. He recalled how Mommy didn't question Daddy about his outside behaviors, she just remained his wife. We told him about how the DNA results are saying that on Mommy's side of the family, Roy and I are on two different generational lines. We explained how that means that my birth mother could possibly be the daughter of one of Mommy's first cousins, and through the process of elimination, it's looking like her Cousin Daisy's daughter.

He remembered them well. He immediately defended Daddy. He said Daddy would never touch a kid; he was into curves. He loved big boobs and a big ass, especially a big ass! He motioned with his arms and hands extended as he spoke on it. Roy agreed, saying yeah, "I was six and I was running around with him. He had lots of chicks! Daddy would never do anything like that." I sat quietly listening to these two men speak on a topic that they had full biases of. First, Mommy did not fit that description at all. She was petite her whole life. And secondly, chicks as in cheating? As my Godfather took his trip down memory lane, my mind took me back to the time Daddy spent in prison. I thought about how intelligent he was because of all the reading and writing he did for years.

We stayed and chatted a little while longer, and I still didn't feel that my inquiry was settled. Until then, the idea that perhaps I was Daddy's only child, hadn't entered my mind. We agreed that Mommy and Daddy had a secret between them, and it could potentially go to the grave. I told him that I would keep him posted on the DNA results as soon as they come in and then we said our goodbyes. He later sent me a text message.

It read, "I'm really happy to see how full and happy your life is, your father loved you and bringing you home proves how much".

I said, "WHAT!?"

The fact that someone was finally able to see what I thought I was seeing for my whole life, was enough to invoke a downpour of happy tears. I didn't worry about how he left out the part of exactly where Daddy brought me home from. He's still an OG and he ain't snitching! I feel Daddy's love to this day! He intentionally and unintentionally taught me so much during the most important era of my life. The treatment I endured over the years pushed me to be who I am today. When I felt rejected, I looked to God. Mommy literally taught me that. I give thanks for that to this day, and that's why no matter how this situation ends, I will always have love and respect for her. As far as that goes, she did her job!

Daddy's youngest and last surviving brother had recently passed during that time. He had a wife and one son who lived near him in his hometown. He did the strangest thing right before his passing. He lived in South Carolina for several years and he visited us in Baltimore periodically throughout the years. Every time he came to town, he would stop by Mommy's house and visit with Risha.

The last time he came up, they took a photo in Mommy's front yard. In the photo there was Risha, Uncle, Risha's only child, and Risha's two grandkids. Uncle returned to his hometown of South Carolina and posted the picture on his social media page as his cover picture. Not soon after, we got word that he had passed away after a long battle with colon cancer. We didn't even know he was sick. From the photo, one couldn't help but notice the striking resemblance they all had. Risha looked more like Uncle than his own son. Risha was about eight months old when I was conceived, and based on her birthday she was conceived when, Tab swears, Daddy was in jail the whole time. Oh boy! I can see me as the problem at that point, because now I just learned another secret! My mind is screaming, **WOODEN NICKELS!** Could this be it? Risha could have had an UncleDaddy? Wow! Still waiting for DNA results, I studied pictures and discovered unimaginable similarities between my cousins and myself. More similarities than I have ever experienced between China and Risha. It was different. I seemed to belong a part of their circle.

Chapter 34 Exhibit B

Finally, round three of DNA results are in. I was expecting to learn that I had a half-sister, but instead it revealed that Robin and I shared very little DNA, which meant that we were not related as half-sisters. In fact, the amount of DNA shared between us was so little, we fell on the category for fourth cousins. I was so confused. I had practically convinced myself that I found my birthmother. I was wrong again. I wanted to give up and just accept things as they were. Accept the confusion and dismay. I was grateful for where I am in life. Is it so important to have closure on this?

Then I scrolled through the pictures in my phone and came across the 'maybe me' baby picture again. I zoomed in and stared into her eyes. I said a quiet prayer and then I said," Ok." It's time to mention the picture to Robin. Pink and I called her to confirm some things. We asked her why did they think that Cousin Daisy was on the photo?

She replied, "It has always been here, and I assumed it was grand mommy because of her birthmark on her chin."

I shook my brain and yelled, "WHAT?"

She said yeah, "grand mommy had a birthmark on her chin that she covered with makeup."

I couldn't breathe. I fought back tears as my voice began to shake, I said to her, "You mean like mines?"

She looked into the camera at my birthmark, paused, and said, "Yes."

"No f*ckin way!"

"Are you sure?"

She said yes, "I know every inch of grand mommy's body, and she had that birthmark on her chin."

I noticed her eyes filling up too. I pointed out the differences in the two photos. She agreed that the baby on the photo was me and not her grandmother.
She asked, "So wait, did grand mommy give a baby away?" I said, "it looks like she could be my grandmother too, but how?"

Robin mentioned the Kelly, who is her aunt. She told me that the two sisters were one year apart in age. I always thought they had a wider age gap between them for some reason. This is where it gets more interesting. I never suspected Kelly to have any involvement because I assumed that we were too close in age for her to be considered. However, she was the person with all the information, including possession of the baby picture. The two of us looked a lot alike. We have an unusual number of similarities. We had no contact for decades. I didn't even recognize her government name when she sent me the friend request a few years earlier. I had to ask Cousin Lia who she was before I accepted it because Cousin Lia was listed as a mutual friend. We became friends on social media, and I begin to take notice to her post. I noticed that she waited until very late in age to have her only son. She was currently unmarried like me. We attended the same college during the same years, and I didn't realize it. I saw the original post of the baby picture. I still felt that it wasn't my place to tell her that she could be mistaken about her own mother. I never did. Her son is thirty years younger than me, but he looks a lot like my sons and grandsons. I heard from other cousins, that he was a handful growing up. Nonetheless, she was now the number one suspect in this.

I started to recall the facts. I took a more intentional look into her social media. From the looks of it, she has been dropping these hints for quite some time. I'm not sure what went on or what may still be going on, but I believed that she had answers. I saw a picture of her father and her sisters by another mother. They all look like me. I understand having the features she inherited from her mother, but her dad too. Is she my cousin, sister, or mother? I have no idea of how this could turn out. I went to my own social media page and reviewed some my older post and noticed that she had commented on a few of them. She seemed to admire my photos in an intimate way as if we were close in real life. I posted an old picture of me at the age of about ten, and she commented, "Awww, so pretty" It may seem innocent or like a normal response to other friends, but it hit me differently. I wondered what she saw when she looked at my picture. Did she realize the resemblance? Is she thinking what I'm thinking? When I look at her pictures, I see my eyes in hers. I wanted to talk to her so bad, but I didn't have the courage. She would have extremely young when I was born, but God! Which would explain the secrecy of my birthmother if she was. I could be way off here. I'm only speculating based on the facts. Unfortunately, the facts lean her way more than Mommy's.

According to the DNA results, Cousin Lia and I are related by way of her grandfather. This was strange because as far as we know, we are first cousins because our mothers are sisters and Tab is their mother. Our common ancestor should be Tab especially since her DNA is in the mix of results now. Her grandfather, Aunt Judy's dad, was the son of one of Tab's half-sisters from her father. The DNA results revealed that Aunt Judy is a product of kissing cousins. The two of them were half first cousins. Cousin Lia couldn't believe the news. She called Tab and asked her if it was true.

   Tab said, "yes, it is." with no problem.

   She said, back then, people were just people. She is ninety-four years old to this date. The results had Tab as my 2nd great grand aunt, and her sister as my great grandmother. We were all confused.

Then one day a representative from the DNA testing company contacted me and asked for an interview. I thought Oh my God! They know something! I accepted the invite. I was surprised that it was zoom meeting scheduled in the next 24 hours. I thought the urgency of it all was confirmation that I was finally waiting to receive. The interview came. I had my grandson next to me recording the whole thing with my cell phone. I pulled the zoom link up on my laptop screen. The interview went on for a little over an hour. The question started out very generic and then some marketing stuff. We then went onto navigating around the DNA website. In my account, one of the features had been stuck on update for several weeks. It was the one that shows your ancestral lines leading back to generations. The information is based on information from the family tree that I build from my own knowledge and my DNA matches. The disclaimer is that the information accrued, does not apply if matches are related in more than one way.

We pulled up a fake account and used it to sample the navigation features. I noticed that the fake names where very close to the names in my real account tree. I caught on to what they were doing. I had the membership for a few months now and I had hundreds of hints that had yet to be explored. I was overwhelmed by the amount, and I couldn't decipher what mattered in my search. The representative, who was a certified genealogist, guided me through the site. The interview ended and it wasn't what I'd hoped for but still very helpful. I was able to go to my actual page try out some of the navigation tools that he showed me. It takes 24 hours for the lines to update once changes are made to your family tree on the site. If it seems correct, the lines will update. If somethings way off, it will not. We decided to try some experimenting.

For weeks, I had Mommy and Daddy listed on my family tree as my parents. My lines never updated. After I changed Mommy's name to Kelly's name, my lines updated. Not just on my account, Cousin Lia saw changes to the lines on her account as well. We were all in shock. This is it we thought. But something still lingered. The DNA results didn't make sense. I didn't know what to do next. We dug deeper into the DNA results and discovered a lot of discrepancies about our family history. The records were conflicting and there was no certainty about who fathered and mothered who in some cases. This whole thing has spent out of control. I didn't know what to think. Cousin Lia started spending less time engaging with me about. Then one day she admits that she secretly had Mommy consent to taking a DNA test.

At first, I felt betrayed because she was making moves like that without my knowledge. She reassured me that she didn't want me to mess things up by saying something before she was able to collect Mommy's sample. It still didn't sit right with me.

I asked," What else have you decided to do without my knowledge?" Cousin Lia said, "nothing. We're just going to wait for her results to come in."

Chapter 35 I Asked God

Weeks passed. This would have to be the final round of testing. I was running out of steam with it all. While waiting on the test results, Mommy continued to limit contact with me. I was convinced that she was finally ready to admit the truth to me. I was hoping that she would tell me respectfully instead of having me see the results of a DNA test.

I planned on spending the entire summer in Baltimore. I needed some real family time. As soon as the school year ended, I packed up my things, and headed up to Baltimore. I was there for a few days before Pink, her best friend, and I hopped on a plane for a girl's trip to Las Vegas. We had just settled into our hotel room when Mommy's DNA results came in. Seeing them was bittersweet.

My initial reaction was shock. The DNA results said Mommy and I shared an enormous amount of DNA and with that considered she can only be matched as my mother. From the inside looking out, there was more to it, but I accepted the results at that time. I started hearing rumors about Mommy being physically affected by all the drama. I heard from my niece that she seemed to be slowing down and forgetting lot of things. She was also disappointed in me for not taking her word for what she said.

I felt heavy with guilt and confusion. Deep down inside of me, I was aching with confusion. I called her as soon as I read the results, to let her know and to apologize. When I called her, she was very surprised to hear what I had to say and reluctant to accept it. It seemed like she didn't believe it herself.

I said, "Hi Mommy! I got your results back. It's over now."
Mommy paused and slowly replied, "you're like that little bird on the cartoon that flies aaallll the way up into the tree only to come crashing down to the ground."
She motioned slowly with her arms and hands as she burst into laughter. I don't know why I would expect anything else. I never spoke to her on the topic again.

    A few weeks later, Cousin Lia through a family cookout on fourth of July to kick off the summer break. Everyone was in attendance including Mommy, Aunt Jane, and Aunt Judy. Tab, and my formerly suspected birth mother cousin Kelly, and her son attended as well. I hadn't seen them in years. I watched her and she watched me. I noticed the resemblance even more now that she was in person. We were the same everything, height, complexion, body type, even our voices had the same pitch. It was creepy.

    We mingled and landed in a corner alone. Me, her, and her son. We stood there in a close circle talking. I didn't know if I was talking with my mother and brother, sister and nephew, or cousins. They both stared at me the whole time like they were examining my features. The conversation was light, mostly about achievements and goals. The son was very eager to share things with me. He seemed proud to let me know that his birthday was just four days before mines yet 30 years apart and our names have the same initials. I didn't have the courage to ask her anything, I just listened. We wrapped up our conversation and I went on with the partying. I couldn't unsee how they both stared so deeply onto my eyes. Maybe they were in aw over the resemblance I have with Cousin Daisy.

Some other cousins told me that Mommy was watching us interact when we were over in the corner, and she seemed to become uneasy. They could have been being messy though.

A few hours later when things were winding down, a line for the closest restroom had formed. Cousins were asking who's in there? No one seemed to know. Everyone waited several more minutes for the restroom to become available. Finally, Kelly emerged. She looked like she had been praying or crying or both. She was in the restroom for a long time, and she was quiet. Before leaving for the evening, we exchanged phone numbers and promised to keep in touch with one another.

When I left, I received a text message from her that read, "Hey Cherry, it was good seeing and talking with you. I'm going to keep in touch."
I replied, "Likewise."

We haven't spoken since, but I continued to get likes and comments to post on my social media page from her. From the inside looking out, I know we'll meet again someday. I returned home to Georgia, and I tried to resume my newfound life, but I was so distracted with home back in Baltimore.

I prayed about it and one day God led me to check out the teacher vacancies there. I saw so many; I couldn't decide on the ones could possibly be a good fit.
I said, "here we go again God. What do you want me to do now?"

I looked up at my laptop and saw an ad for a leadership role in Special Education. I read the details of the position, and it was exactly what I was currently doing in Georgia with a little more razzle dazzle of course. However, it matched my qualifications, and the position was one that I had always wanted. I submitted my resume. When I received the invitation to interview, I already knew that I would be packing my bags. God has a way of not only telling me exactly what to do, but he also shows me when to do it! I prayed for a reset, and was promoted into the position, that at the start of my career was my long-term goal, The IEP Chair!

When I told Cason the news, he said, "Wow, grandma, you're so blessed! I knew God would see that you did that!" I agreed.

After spending four years in another state, returning home I must have experienced the same feeling people have when retuning from college or the military. I had learned so much and gained a lot of insight, but I still felt confused about my own story. The confusion went from seeking information to what to do with the information now that it had been discovered. Reflecting on the sermon, I replayed it again. This time I listened to it from a different perspective. I was seeking answers. I prayed about the whole series of events. I realized that the story was my own. Being back in my hometown made things clear. Everything was starting to click for me, and adjusting to myself existing in the city without LB and Cousin Tricie was my biggest struggle.

Chapter 36 What a Friend

I made an abrupt late entry into the school year to fill a leadership role at an urban elementary school. I was the newest Chairperson overseeing the operations of the special education department. Complete with my own office and an assistant to handle most of the administrative responsibilities. I chaired the meetings for a team of professionals to include social workers, phycologist, advocates, educators, therapist, and more. I was met with that good ole Bmore careful welcome. The job came with an enormous amount of responsibility. I had to get right into correcting errors while making my own along way. The team had opinions of me from the start. From the inside looking out, God was still guiding my steps. One team member told me that I needed to earn my likes before I could expect the team to have a positive response to me. The following week, another team member came into my office to let me know that she overheard everything, *apologized* on the team's behalf, and recommended that I conduct a restart. She suggested that I pretty much allow the team to run the department in the same manner as it was before I assumed the position. She so eloquently stated that she had a lot of clout, and she *really* wanted me to be there next year. Before either of them made their statements, my new direct report to person had already shared his warning, advising me to basically leave his team alone because he's not losing anyone. At the same time, the person designated as my specialist, went out for an extended period. To top it all off, my assistant also went out on an extended leave. By the end of my second month, I was placed on an action plan. My direct report to person, sent the email along with news of my assistant being permanently pulled from my office to work in a classroom due to teacher shortages. Paperwork was out of order and before I could put anything in proper order, response to the notice of intent for the upcoming school year email was due. I was in the thick of things with no direction, story of my life. I thought, here I go again God. I somehow managed to show my hand. I was struggling with all the new discoveries, and it was weighing me down. I didn't realize that maybe I was given off the wrong energy. I prayed about it daily. I needed God to please provide me with direction. I wasn't comfortable in my mind space. I felt alone in my own work home. However, I knew that my real team was with me every day! God had shown me enough times over, that I had absolutely nothing to fear!

  Two days before we were getting off for Christmas break, God sent me another message. This time, it was delivered in hand by way of another stranger who worked as a teacher. It had been a long month. I hadn't left the building for the day, and I was already overwhelmed for what I would be returning to after the break. The teacher participated in the schools secret Santa and my assistant was his partner to exchange gifts with. He came by the office looking for her while she was still out on leave. That was that first time that we had met. We spoke briefly and I mentioned that I was working on a project. He could sense the intensity. He said that in his spare time, he did crafts. He shared a story with me about a situation he experienced a few months earlier and because of the experience he was left with an item that he made. He said God told him to give it to me because it was for me, not for the person he thought it was intended.
He said, "you're a believer, a follower of Christ."

He said as he stood there speaking with me, he felt chills through his body. From the inside looking out, he could sense anointment. The next day, he came back to my office with a huge gift bag containing a big, wrapped box. It was heavy and solid. He asked me not to open it until Christmas. I agreed.

On Christmas morning, I said my prayers and starting busying around the house in preparation for the festivities expected. I had the music for the season playing. I grabbed the gift just as everyone started to come down to the tree. It was heavy and everyone wanted to know what was inside. I removed the large heavy wrapped square shaped box. It had a red ribbon tied around it with a bow. I untied the bow and open the flaps on the box. There was another box inside. I paused and thought, um, it's in original packaging. It was taped with clear tape along the seams, I cut the tape and revealed a third box.
Now I'm thinking, "oh...this is a gag gift."
I laughed and I almost set it aside for later, but it was so heavy. I had to see what was weighing it down so much. I cleared away the access wrapping and I had just the single box on my lap. I shook it a little and I didn't hear a thing. I opened it partially. This time I saw a flat piece of wood. I thought it's still a gag, the wood was weighing it down. I opened it completely, and I was flabbergasted! It was a huge handmade perfectly crafted circle, made from high quality solid wood. It had a bible verse Matthew 6:33-34, carved into it.
Carved across the top in deep bold letters it read, "ON GOD'S TIME".

I just held it close and smiled because I knew it was more confirmation. From the inside looking out, my work situation was no more difficult than that hike through the snow with Daddy back in the day. I was more than ready for the challenge. The whole situation was another distraction to throw me off course. I knew who sent me there, and I would miraculously come out of it on top. This would not be just another win; this was a part of my story. I could only trust God to continue writing it.

Then what happened next made it the most epic Christmas that I will always remember! I tapped on my social media icon to check out the affirmations from people who were also up. While scrolling through the threads, I didn't notice anything that I found interesting. It made me think about what I posted last. I went to my profile. I hadn't posted anything since throwback Thursday a few weeks earlier. I chuckled at myself. It was a picture of me from elementary school on picture day. I noticed that my eyes still looked like the eyes on the baby picture. The discovery led me to go to the actual picture that I had saved in the photo library on my phone. Before that moment, I had never looked past the mushroom hairdo I had in the picture. But on this day, I zoomed in. What I noticed left me speechless. It was the final piece of confirmation that I needed to positively identify me in the infamous baby picture.

On the baby picture, all the light spots are clearly shown including the one below my left eye covering the entire lower eyelid. In the photo where I was ten years old, my complexion had darkened to light brown however, the same light spots still showed through. As I got older, my birthmark faded in some areas. That same spot was still clear on my left eye at the age of ten. I recalled the teasing back in elementary school.

I remembered how I prayed to God many times to make it go away. It wasn't until that moment when I realized that God literally hid the light spots on my face from me just as I prayed for.

I had forgotten the mark was there and had to look for it! I could not help but to give God the glory in that moment, because he was blessing me with answers to my prayers all along. I ran to the bathroom mirror, turned on the light, and checked my face. The light spot below my lower left eyelid was still there, perfectly blended into my complexion! I got the absolute best gift ever! **ANSWERS!** This Christmas, I positively identified my baby picture. Not an ounce of doubt about it!

Doing so gave me closure to a lifelong inquiry. It was truly a blessing that I am so grateful to have received. God is amazing! I didn't know it then but, God knew that my birthmark would serve this purpose on his time!

I was overwhelmed with questions and answers, my mind raced. I felt like wooden nickels were being flicked off at me one after another.
I asked God, "Why?

I had finally reached the part where I got the answer to a question that I have being seeking over the course of my entire life. I talked to God about all of it to reached understanding and direction. From the inside looking out, I accepted that I was born into an unfavorable situation and how I was perceived a problem. I knew that I spent time with my praying birth mother in the beginning; someone cared for me because they had me professionally photographed when I was an infant. I knew that Mommy was not that person, by her own admittance and because of her inability to identify me on my baby picture. It took quite a while to process that part. How could she allow me to go my entire life asking questions about my birthmark and never once mention that her close first cousin had a matching one.

I replayed situations from as early as I could remember, and things started to click together like an oversized wooden puzzle that formed a Big Wooden Nickel. I thought about how disregarded and discarded I felt growing up. How much I longed for validation. Challenged to learn things the hard way, unintentionally overachieving and suffering guilt due to the lack of acknowledgements on achievements, or celebrations of successes. I learned to be ashamed of wins because I was surrounded by loses. A lifetime of figuring it out as it happens because there has never been any clear direction from the people who were in place to be the influence. The people who were the model for me to follow, led me to believe that my best is not enough. I understood how everything that I experienced over my lifetime had prepared me for this moment. The moment of truth.

I went back to the beatings and wondered how many of them were given out of malice because of who they knew I was. I was devastated thinking about how Mommy and Daddy must have felt watching me grow into an exact replica of something they both wanted to forget. I understood the beatings. All of them! I thought about how they had to lead people on as we got older and developed into our own looks, how they always had to explain me. Mommy would say things like, "she likes to eat, or she's the hardheaded one", to explain my size or my behavior. I thought about how I had to tuck in my feelings about things that hurt me because expressing those feelings would amount to more things that hurt me, and how I never felt supported. What were they thinking!?

From the inside looking out, I imagined how Daddy developed the plan. He was always in game mode. He was intelligent, manipulative and the product of his environment. Mommy looked at me in the same disappointed way she looked at him sometimes. He must have become a master of deception while in prison. It would not surprise me if my baby picture originated from his side of the family.

I remember what he said to me often. He told me that I was different and that I would someday understand why. I believe that at some point during his numerous stays in prison, he talked to God. He knew he did some bad things. The riddles and clues embedded in the song lyrics he loved so much couldn't hold a candle to his ace in the hold. Knowledge of my baby picture all along. Solid clues provided a cogent argument for me when I finally reached the capacity to properly handle it. It, being the biggest wooden nickel that I could only imagine.

I went back to me telling Mommy about the results of the DNA test and how disconnected from her I felt after watching her reaction to the news. When confronted, how she went on a rant about doing all the work, and spending her money, but never mentioned anything about pregnancy or labor. I thought about how this woman raised me. I watched her cook, clean, work, earn her education, raise grandkids, support strangers, and conduct herself as a devoted child of God. The same woman instilled my values, taught me how to pray, how to read, clean, cook, and conduct myself as a positive member of society. Still in disbelief, "Why would she continue to deny my truth?"

As sure as I wanted to be, I couldn't ignore the small amount of doubt that still lingered. My thoughts wouldn't rest with confusion about the DNA results. I knew there had to be more to this.

Chapter 37 Imagine Me

New Year's 2024 came in, I thought more and more about the DNA results, so I went back to revisit the website. It had been a few months since I'd last checked for updates. I wasn't looking for anything, but I noticed the hints light blinking and all my close matches had footnotes. I started clicking. I followed the clicks which took me deeper and deeper into my ancestral lines. Many close family members posted details about the family's history, making the experience feel like I was attending my family reunion right alongside my ancestors. I read though countless records such as census reports, military draft cards, marriage and divorce certificates, birth and death records, burial sites, and more. I reviewed photos posted by family members, year books, and other family member's family trees. I belong to a huge family! I was able to trace my ancestral lines back as far as five generations and discovered that the average family household sizes where in the double digits. As I continued learning about my ancestral lines, I noticed something disturbing.

In many instances, Mommy wasn't showing up in my ancestral line. Tab was related to me as my great grand aunt, and distant cousin from other lines. After further inquiry, I discovered that, Mommy and Cousin Lia's mother, both appeared on different ancestral lines than Tab in some instances. Could this possibly mean that Tab is not either one of their birth mothers? I was floored again! This would explain the lack of affection throughout our family. Mommy couldn't give me what she never had, because a mother's love didn't come naturally for her. I was a business not a baby, because so was she.

I reviewed the facts by further exploration of the generations before Tab's mother. That's when I discovered an alarming pattern! Generations of family members were repeatedly marrying and producing children among one another. Tab was one of fifteen kids, some of them were born as the product of their other family members. Her siblings had kids in high numbers as well. Some of them had as many twenty or more children in one household, and they helped one another out with raising them. Tab always says people were just people then. That was her unapologetic explanation when Cousin Lia and I informed her of how we'd discovered that Cousin Lia's grandfather was her half-sister's son. In all the years, that fact was never known by anyone in my generation. Things clicked for me even more. Tab's response reminded me that she too could keep secrets. Cousin Lia took it for face value, but I felt that it was a wooden nickel that lacked a little polish.

From the inside looking out, I understood how they earned the title, "silent generation". We discovered that Aunt Judy wasn't the only family member born from mating within. Our family's DNA results were like a textbook example of not only isolated occurrences of pedigree collapse, but also endogamy. Pedigree collapse is one or few isolated incidents of cousin marriage. Endogamy is when cousin marriage occurs repeatedly over many, many, generations. The effect of this phenomenon on our DNA matches provided me with the final piece of confirmation that I needed. The overall effect of endogamy is to make many of our DNA matches appear to more closely related than they really are. This is because the total amount of shared chromosomes will reflect extra, to include all the many ways of relatedness. The DNA company's predicted relatedness is not applicable in cases of pedigree collapse, endogamy, or multiple ways of relatedness.

According to the DNA testing companies and other sources, my close family members married one another and bared children together repeatedly generations and generations before me. Like a wooden nickel, our DNA results cannot be taken for face value because the number of shared chromosomes are inflated. In fact, they are of no use in confirming the true relatedness between Mommy and me.

That was all she had left to stand on, and it crumbled when the DNA confirmed evidence of endogamy. The large amount of DNA shared between us represented the total amount of chromosomes from all combined lines. From the inside looking out, it finally made sense. To this day, the "silent generation", continue to keep quiet.

I wondered if Mommy knew this all along about herself and if that caused her reactions to my questions. Then I wondered if her not knowing caused her reactions to my questions. Either way, I understood why she saw me as a "Problem".

I always asked questions. I couldn't relax without understanding the why in situations. I needed things to make sense! I consistently prayed for answers. Little did I know, every experience was an intended lesson. Even the ones embedded with distractions meant to change my trajectory, forced me to make choices and decisions while preparing me for this moment. The moment of truth. My truth, from the inside looking out.

My truth from the inside looking out is that I lived my entire life as a stranger to myself. What I perceived as a lifetime of unfair treatment, judgement, discard, disrespect, lies, and tricks, was fuel required to ignite this fire!

God has surely guided my steps. My truth is that my story is an example of how God's power works! My life experiences were repeated proof of God's presence. I was led to my truth by keeping my faith in God. I chose the path intended, and that's why God chose me. My truth is affirmed in the lessons that I have learned through my own personal experiences which repeated the experiences of my ancestors. My <u>truth</u> is the elixir required to break the generational curse's that has held my family in bondage for centuries.

My birth mother's identity has not been confirmed nor denied. Which is what makes me believe that if she were alive, she will reveal herself someday. I forgave her and I pray that she can forgive me. I could only imagine the lifelong trauma she had to suffer with all of this. The thought of me being a trigger, keeps me from outright asking the only other cousin who I suspect knows the truth. I know that my birth was not the typical birth. That alone makes me a miracle baby! I recognized me in the mirror after years of trying to see someone else's reflection. My feelings were finally validated! I put all the feelings associated with that old confused, rejected, disregarded, disrespected, disappointed version of me into one bag, drowned them in their own tears, and tossed them out! God had his hands on me since before my arrival. He sent me a direct message. I didn't understand it then, but I understood now.

Two years had passed, and a lot of changes occurred. In the message, the Pastor said that I was Chosen. I was confused about what I was chosen to do. I listened again, with intention on learning what my next steps should be, I got it!

The title of the sermon was, "You Are the One". The text was taken from the Bible book 1 Peter 2:4 - 10. The pastor said, "Your story will no longer be a secret, have you ever noticed you hide your pass from yourself because you're so ashamed of it?"

"No longer are you permitted to be ashamed of your pass."

He continued along those lines and then he said somethings that I was hearing for the very first time.

He said, "These strangers have had an experience with God *'Cherry'* that has put them in position to be a witness to others about what only God can do."
He continued, "the world needs to know what God can do." "Your story is a bridge for breakthrough for the broken, a seed of salvation for the loss, a path to purpose for the person without vision."

The pastor ended that sermon by saying, "Say self, look at you...I am walking unapologetically in my purpose! If folks only knew the cost of the oil on my life!"

I did just that! My next steps were laid out for me as always, as my story goes. I thought back to when I met with that Pastor two years earlier. From the inside looking out, I was transformed into the person that I was created to be. I looked different. I thought differently. I prayed differently. I was comfortable and secure with me. I learned that through all my experiences, I prayed. I prayed for forgiveness if I thought that I forgot to pray! I know God heard me because he continued to show me through the blessings that I consistently received. I give God all the Glory, in Jesus' name.

I held on to the lessons. The biggest lesson learned was that I must trust God in Jesus' name through all things. I learned to trust and believe that my God is the mighty God able to heal my heart with clarity and understanding and overflowing forgiveness. Looking back, I realize that nothing in my life happened to me, but everything happened for me. When I thought I was calling on God, God was calling on me. I am thankful to have heard the call. Through knowledge and understanding, I was able to forgive Mommy, Daddy, and my generations before me. I understand how the behaviors and practices cycled all the way through them, resulting in their decision making and actions. That's what makes the Nickel Wooden! I forgave because I am forgiven.

From the inside looking out I saw Daddy struggle with his own issues as a young immature boy trapped inside of a grown man's body. Most of his life with me occurred while he was in prison. However, he was able to provide me with important life lessons, never losing an ounce of respect from me during that time. I don't know who he had as role models because his father nor his brothers were career criminals. Daddy had a different path than his siblings. Somewhere along the way, he was attached to this assignment. That's his story, and that's what I had to first accept. I thought about all the talks we had, and how he always kept me on my toes with riddles that invoked critical thinking. He often reminded me that I was built different and how important it was to not take wooden nickels for face value. He made sure I knew that I was the apple of his eyes. I could forgive Daddy for how he raised me because I know that I got the best parts of him when I needed him most. The bond that Daddy and I shared would not have existed had he not been incarcerated during my most impressionable years. He learned how to play the hand he was delt. I know this to be true based on all the times when "the street him" didn't like me and when "the street me", didn't like him right back. Many times, I had to ask God how was I supposed to honor thy father when he ain't showing me that he is worthy to be honored?

I remembered praying, "...but God, please forgive him."

I learned that forgiveness was the answer. I forgave him for raising me from prison for the first twelve years of my life, me never realizing that he wouldn't get twelve more. I thought about how I didn't even realize he was in prison for many years because of how much he controlled our thinking. I forgave him for losing his battle with drug addiction and contracting that terminal illness by my fifteenth birthday. I forgave him for leaving this earth when I was just eighteen, and before he reached the age of forty. Never meeting his first grandsons, cheating them out of that relationship; I forgave him for missing my college graduations and my weddings. I forgave him for not being here now so that I could tell him that I figured out the wooden nickels' thing.

Most importantly, I forgave him for keeping the secret. The secret was deeply camouflaged in a nest of perfect situations all conducive to the immense value of *his* wooden nickel. Daddy's secret was dark. He was 22 years old when I was born. God made my light shine right through it! I forgave because I was able to understand Daddy's predicament. He could he never tell me the story of my conception without shame. I was a living breathing constant reminder of his biggest mistake. I processed how he must have felt knowing that at his most vulnerable time, his faith was tested. He had to literally live with his mistake for the rest of his life. I remember when things switched up in our relationship. How much I wanted to redeem myself during that time because Daddy 's love for me made a drastic change. He wanted me gone in real life, right around the time he got diagnosed with his illness. That alone, kept me on my toes.

Mommy suffered through all this too. From the inside looking out, she accepted me as her own and even after my father's death, was forced to continue protecting the narrative that became her reality. I forgave Mommy for her suffering in silence all those years of trying to love me without knowing how or why. I forgave Mommy for not asking questions that needed to be answered and for not answering questions that were asked. My mind still not quite settled with how do I accept all of this? I had to allow logic to prevail. It's quite possible that Mommy had no idea who my birth mother was and couldn't identify me in the baby picture because for whatever reason, she hadn't seen me at that age. Could it be that Daddy never revealed her identity until he determined my permanent placement? As far as I can tell, Mommy had the same questions that I had and was as interested in knowing the truth as me too. That was all that I could expect from her. She didn't know where I came from, she just knew she had to accept me. She couldn't answer my questions detailing my birth because she didn't have the answers. I forgave her for allowing herself to be manipulated by Daddy and for not forgiving herself for choices made that she knew were mistakes. The thoughts of her being consumed in this falsehood forced me to pray for her healing. I forgave her for never being able to admit my truth to me. I understand that she has her own assignment from God too. God still provided filters for her to make sure that I had access to him, as she was supposed to.

I could recognize where I had experienced situations that I know only God saw me through. Mommy showed me the way to him, as her first order of business despite whatever Daddy had going on. She spent countless nights with us, on our knees in prayer from as early as I could recall. No matter what went on around us, from the inside looking out, she put God first in all things. My faith was built from those foundational years, and I relied heavily on that faith. Times when distractions came my way, God took the wheel with or without my knowledge. I trust him. I no longer accept the lifelong label of the problem. I embrace the fact that I am indeed the <u>solution!</u>

May God continue to bless my family.

Meet: Charity *<u>Heal</u>*!

Epilogue

My Life, My Story.

My story is intended to demonstrate how my relationship with God has always been the one solid thing in my life. I am grateful to be a witness to God's power and I am so glad he chose me to live my life and to tell my story.

Acknowledgement

My family, close and distant. Morning Star Baptist Church of Baltimore MD, Urban Teachers of Baltimore, MD, The Kindezi Schools of Atlanta Georgia, Sojourner Douglass College of Baltimore Maryland, Baltimore City Public Schools, and all my sandbox friends.

Special thanks to

My students, Educators, colleagues, mentors, and other chosen strangers.

WOODEN NICKELS, The Inside Looking Out

www.ingramcontent.com/pod-product-compliance
Lightning Source LLC
Chambersburg PA
CBHW060949230426
43665CB00015B/2125